The Unwritten
The Unspoken

What's this life for?

By Kevin Scroggins

The Unwritten - The Unspoken:
What's this life for?

ISBN Paperback: 979-8-89576-112-0
ISBN Hardback: 979-8-89576-113-7

Published by:

This book is dedicated to my mother, father, brothers, children, and small nucleus of friends. Without you, I would not be where I am today. You are my greatest inspiration. You are the reason I strive for greatness every day, to leave a legacy for you to be proud of.

Always proud of you, forever here for you.

Table of Contents

Introduction

Welcome to my journey of resilience, self-discovery, and transformation. I'm excited to share my story with you, not just as a narrative of challenges and triumphs but as a testament to the power of perseverance.

Born in 1971, I grew up in a modest neighborhood, raised by a Marine and Vietnam veteran father, who dedicated 35 years to serving as a police officer, and a hardworking mother who drove a school bus. As the eldest of three boys, I often felt the weight of responsibility, particularly when my childhood took unexpected turns. I faced challenges with attention deficit issues, which led to transitions between public and private schools, leaving me feeling as though I was struggling to keep pace with my peers. These experiences instilled in me a foundation of resilience that would prove crucial as I navigated life's ups and downs.

Let me clarify what I am not: I am not special by any stretch of the imagination. I'm not famous or well-known in Hollywood, nor did I rise from a privileged background. My mother even sewed tiny horses onto my shirts to give the illusion of affording Polo—now I proudly own twenty of them, just for the sake of it. I come from humble beginnings, perhaps much like yours, and from the start, the odds were stacked against me. Demographically and statistically, I was not expected to succeed, especially to the extent that my life and career have flourished. I am an ordinary person who has faced significant challenges and transformed those struggles into an extraordinary, fulfilling life. My journey is a testament to the power of resilience and the potential within each of us to rise above our circumstances.

Adversity was a constant companion—temptations and obstacles shaped my formative years. High school introduced me to the pitfalls of alcohol and drugs. Instead of succumbing to these temptations, I fought my way through, emerging stronger and more determined. My college years were no less tumultuous; I faced legal troubles that led to my expulsion, yet I refused to let that define me. Working during the day at a county park while attending night classes, I ultimately earned my degree from the University of Houston. Each challenge became a stepping stone, reinforcing my belief in the power of perseverance. What more powerful example of perseverance than beating cancer twice!

I have become a self-made millionaire, proudly raised three wonderful children, and ventured into entrepreneurship, serving as the company president while owning three other companies. My path has been anything but traditional; it has been a winding maze filled with unforeseen challenges and invaluable lessons that have shaped my character and outlook on life, taking me from the ordinary to the extraordinary.

Beyond my professional achievements, I am deeply committed to giving back to the community. I founded Santa's Elves, a nonprofit inspired by the belief that 'to whom much is given, much will be required' (Luke 12:48). Our team of founders, volunteers, and sponsors dedicate their time and resources to support local organizations and individuals. Since our launch, we have raised over $1.5 million to assist those in need, including cancer survivors, veterans, and neighbors impacted by natural disasters. My experiences have given me a profound appreciation for the resilience of the human spirit, driving my mission to improve lives and serve others. I firmly believe that this is my purpose on Earth.

Throughout my journey, I've absorbed invaluable lessons—many of which aren't found in textbooks or taught by professors; hence, **The Unwritten - The Unspoken**. These principles have shaped my resilience and helped me navigate life's adversities, turning challenges into growth and strength. I've had the privilege of mentoring young people who, like I once was, are searching for direction and purpose.

To achieve anything in life, I believe it's crucial to explore not just what you want to do but who you want to be. This process of self-discovery has helped me define the goals I wanted to achieve and the purpose for my life. The premises and habits I'm eager to share with you are not widely taught; they emerged from my life experiences and lessons learned along the way. These insights have empowered an ordinary young man from an average neighborhood, often told he wouldn't amount to much, to rise above mediocrity and uncertainty. In this book, I aim to share the insights and principles that have guided me, many of which were born from lived experience.

As you embark on this journey with me, I hope you find inspiration and a strong blueprint for living. Together, let's unlock your resilience and turn your challenges into opportunities for growth. I invite you to join me in exploring these transformative principles to help you navigate your winding path to success.

So, if you are soul-searching, trying to understand what this life is for, and looking to recalibrate your life, no matter your age or stage of life, this book is for you. I will provide you with premises, exercises, resources, and inspiration to self-reflect on who you want to be and the framework to help you get there. I guarantee you have not heard, nor will you hear, these ideas taught by a college professor or in traditional academics.

Change is not easy, and rest assured that you do not achieve the life you want by simply wishing or hoping for it to happen. It takes hard work, grit, tenacity, resilience, and sacrifice. It also takes action, which is why I have made this more than another book by a guy claiming to have overcome struggles. I will walk you through the path I took and the premises on which I created the blueprint for my life. Then, I will give you actionable steps that you can take to help you achieve your utopia. But I warn you—this is not for the faint of heart or those who are not self-motivated to put in the effort. I will ask you to take a good, hard look in the mirror!

As I will do throughout these chapters, let me share a story.

One evening, an elderly Cherokee told his grandson about a battle that goes on inside each of us.

He said, "My son, the battle is between two 'wolves' inside us all. One is evil. It is anger, envy, jealousy, sorrow, regret, greed, arrogance, self-pity, guilt, resentment, inferiority, lies, false pride, superiority, and ego.

The other is good. It is joy, peace, love, hope, serenity, humility, kindness, benevolence, empathy, generosity, truth, compassion, and faith.

The same fight is going on inside you—and inside every other person, too."

The grandson thought about it for a minute and then asked his grandfather, "Which wolf wins?"

The old Cherokee simply replied, "**The one that you feed**."

The moral of the story lies in the idea that the wolf you "feed"—through your actions, thoughts, and choices—will grow stronger and define your character, ultimately directing your path. The story emphasizes the importance of personal responsibility in shaping one's mindset and life by focusing on the conscious development of positive traits and values. Throughout this book, I will pull back the covers on how your mindset, thoughts, and choices dictate your actions (or inaction) and give you the tools and resources to take responsibility for feeding the 'good wolf'.

Before we dive in, ask yourself: Are you different from me? Are you ordinary, looking to become extraordinary? Do you know what your life is for? Stick with me as I define the blueprint and premises I have used to feed the joy, peace, love, truth, and humility in my life.

CHAPTER 1

Utopia

It was an early Sunday morning in 1985. My brothers and I were crammed into the backseat of our family's Ram Charger —a vehicle my dad had proudly acquired. We were on our way to church in Cypress, Texas, a weekly ritual that felt both ordinary and monumental. For my family—my father, a police officer, and my mother, a bus driver—dining at Luby's cafeteria after the service was the highlight of our week. It was a simple pleasure, yet it seemed like a feast amid our busy lives.

As I sat there between my younger brothers, trying to keep them from killing each other right there in the back of the truck, my mind wandered to the sermon I would soon hear.

What would the preacher say?

How would his words resonate with me?

I was only 13, but I was already grappling with questions that felt much larger than my young age warranted. That day, the preacher introduced me to the concept of utopia, a concept that I later understood serves as a mindset for life. He explained that utopia was not a tangible reality on Earth. It was a lofty ideal, an imagined place where everything is perfect, yet one that we would never reach since perfection itself is not achievable.

Listening to him, I couldn't help but reflect on the adversities I had already faced. I had encountered struggles that many adults might never experience, including physical and mental abuse. The preacher's words echoed in my mind: utopia is far from achievable. I nodded silently, agreeing with him, yet a flicker of rebellion sparked within me.

Couldn't utopia be more than an unreachable dream or intangible concept?

His sermon got me thinking about what utopia *could* look like if not perfection.

As I got older and my worldview and its possibilities expanded, the notion of utopia began to evolve. I realized it wasn't merely an external place or a distant destination. Utopia was a mindset, a lens through which to view the world. It was about defining what a fulfilling life looked like for me, regardless of external circumstances. It was about setting goals, dreaming big, and setting my life on a course to reach a place that was as close to perfection or utopia as possible.

Now, I want to stress that how I define utopia will certainly not be the same as how you define it. Throughout the following chapters, I will discuss the events, circumstances, and obstacles I experienced that could have derailed me from the vision I hold dear as my utopia. The beauty is that as the concept of utopia evolved in my mind, so did the notion that life will throw you curveballs that will force you to pivot. It does not mean that your vision for utopia is bad or unachievable; it might just mean that you have to follow a different path to get there. As we walk on this journey together, it is imperative that you understand that defining and achieving your utopia is an individualized journey, and what worked for me may not be the same for you.

The premise behind this concept of utopia is that it is a **mindset** to help you achieve what you want in life. So, before we get too far, I want to ask you, based on what I've shared so far, *what utopia means to you.* For some, it may be a peaceful life surrounded by loved ones, while for others, it might involve achieving professional success or contributing to a larger cause. The beauty of utopia lies in its subjectivity. It is not a one-size-fits-all destination but a personal journey that requires introspection and intention. Throughout this book, I will provide you with a plethora of examples of how I traversed life and the pursuit of utopia and how I define it.

Realizing that if I wanted more in my life and to fully step into the life I envisioned, I would have to not only dream big but also establish achievable goals and milestones along the way. I also had to be prepared to face obstacles and barriers and develop a plan to deal with them as they came.

I began this journey by breaking down utopia into five key principles or pillars, which I define using the acronym SPEED: Spiritual, Physical, Emotional, Economic, and Development. Each area serves as a guidepost for my journey, helping me identify actions and habits that align with my vision of a fulfilling life. It is up to you to determine how you define success in each of the SPEED pillars. Although this is my acronym, I encourage you to use this framework to develop one that suits you and your vision of utopia.

As no two people's utopia will ever be exactly the same, it is a defined, individual endeavor—there is no looking to the right or to the left at how other people define their utopia or goals. Your vision for what you want in life may even be counterintuitive to where you came from or where society has deemed you should be going. Your utopia may differ greatly from that of your parents, spouse, or siblings. Although I have drilled this concept into my children's heads for years, each definition of utopia is uniquely theirs.

As you will see, given my middle-class upbringing and average lifestyle, I was not expected to achieve the success I have at this point in my life. My success can only be attributed to my commitment to achieving what I defined as my utopia many years ago.

I have met many people, young and old, who have dreams but have never set any goals as to how to achieve them. Unfortunately, many people wake up one day wondering how they got there without any recollection of the milestones, hurdles, or accomplishments, and many regret not having yet achieved their life's dreams. I refuse to be that person, wandering through life without ambition, desire, or, more importantly, a plan to accomplish all that I want. As the tragedy of life unfolds around us, we must all recognize that our time here is too short to allow life to carry us toward wherever it deems fit.

Before I ask you to define your utopia, we first have to understand what motivates you.

What makes you tick?

What is it that moves you to push forward or toward?

Is it financial success?

Professional achievement?

Personal satisfaction of knowing that you have made a difference?

I argue that you can succeed in these areas, and your motivations and utopia will evolve as you go through experiences and circumstances change. Whether it's the desire for a healthier lifestyle, emotional balance, or the ambition to advance in your career, identifying what drives you will make the journey toward your utopia more meaningful and attainable.

In the hustle and bustle of daily life, it's easy to overlook the importance of pausing to reflect on our goals and aspirations. The sooner we define our utopia, the sooner we can take actionable steps toward achieving it.

What does achievement look like for you in these areas?

Take the time to reflect and write down your visions for each pillar. Once you have clarity, break down the necessary steps to achieve your goals. How many people actually pause and set life goals?

Looking back on that Sunday morning in 1985, I realize it was a pivotal moment.

While the preacher taught that utopia was unattainable, I began to see it as a mindset that could guide my actions and choices. It became clear that while the world may present challenges, our perspective can transform those challenges into opportunities for growth.

To help you understand how to define your utopia, I'll refer to the acronym SPEED along the way and dive into it further in the next chapter. Having a clear path as we navigate this journey together is pivotal, so let me share what SPEED means to me.

I started writing this book during my second bout with cancer, quarantined during the pandemic at MD Anderson and receiving chemotherapy in isolation. It was a time when my life was put into stark perspective. Facing the unknown, I realized that relying solely on external forces for strength was too heavy to bear alone, especially in that dark valley when my fitness in each of my SPEED pillars took a hit.

Let me explain.

My spiritual fitness was ingrained in me from an early age. I hold myself accountable for my morning devotions, attend church on Sundays, and surround myself with a community that holds me accountable for my faith.

As for physical fitness, I have always made sure to remain active. Whether participating in CrossFit, triathlons, or adventure races, I have constantly challenged myself to be physically strong. And as an example of utopia itself being fluid, with each age and stage of life, my physical fitness pivoted. I may not engage in adventure races, but I play pickleball and lift weights, ensuring each task includes repetition and high intensity for my heart! By the time I'm 60, I'm sure there will be something new that catches my interest, and again, I will pivot. The idea is that while I may never achieve perfection in any exercise or regimen, what can I do to get as close as possible?

Economic fitness has always been very high on the priority

list. Because it was important to me, I have identified it as a motivator, and I knew that defining my utopia would include financial success. To achieve this goal, I voraciously read books like *The Wealthy Barber* and *The Millionaire Next Door*, lived below my means, and maximized my 401(k). Taking these steps, I became a millionaire by the time I was 30 years old.

Emotional fitness is about being in tune with our emotions, mental health, and perspective. Like any other muscle, the brain must be exercised and monitored. Regularly checking in with myself and evaluating my mental well-being is paramount to achieving my life's vision. Depression, anxiety, and PTSD are at record highs in our society, partly because mental health issues have gone unchecked and unaddressed for so long. We must keep our finger on the pulse of our mind so that we can allocate more time for self-care, relaxation, and introspection as needed to stay focused on our goals.

Ask yourself: Is your battery fully charged?

Many people are comfortable in the inertia of where they are and, frankly, may have always been. I believe that if you're not moving forward, you are moving backward. And why would I want to be where I was before, not making any progress toward my goals? There is a fine line between comfort and stagnation. I have seen far too many people fall into the latter. They are comfortable with their current life position and circumstances, so they do not put any effort into becoming a better father, son, employee, wife, mother, or leader. This means constantly learning, evaluating, modifying, and changing, with my goal in sight. It also means continually asking myself what I can do today to move forward, making myself better in my roles and on my pillars.

I regularly monitor my progress in each area using a developmental barometer. In other words, where am I in achieving success according to how I defined my utopia? As I mentioned earlier, defining utopia is an individual endeavor, so it is safe to say that each person must have their own **developmental barometer.** You will hear this term mentioned multiple times throughout this book. You must continue to measure yourself in your utopia. This is something that I do every week, month, and year. Why wait for New Year's like so many people do to evaluate where you are in life? To achieve success, you need to do regular check-ins and be ready to pivot.

You may have realized that the concept of utopia is complex and even obtuse. And as humans, we know that achieving **perfection is unparalleled**. In reality, utopia is NOT about perfection at all. It's about defining your utopia and striving to get as close to it as possible. Sadly, most people don't even think about their goals; they only think about their dreams. Many people wake up and realize their dreams have not come to fruition, but it is often too late, especially if they have never taken the time to think about their goals. The sooner you figure out your goals, the more likely you are to achieve your dreams.

It is critical that you remain open and flexible during the process. Of course, once you set your mind toward accomplishing your goals, you want to stay focused on them.

However, life is unpredictable and will throw curveballs, obstacles, and storms preventing you from achieving them. Could this derail you from reaching utopia? For sure—if you let it! I could have allowed having cancer (twice) to deter me from living my life to the fullest. Instead of wallowing in self-pity, regret, and remorse, I had to **shift my utopia** and priorities in how I defined each of my SPEED pillars to accommodate my life circumstances.

In other words, your utopia may change, but the priorities surrounding how you define your pillars should remain constant. When I got cancer for the first time at 29, my economic pillar was heavily weighted; I suddenly realized I had to be a physical and emotional giant. So, my priorities shifted more toward the physical and the emotional pillars.

It is essential to understand that how you define your utopia will determine the level of sacrifice required. You choose the level of sacrifice that you are willing to tolerate. For example, in the medical field, there are surgeons, practitioners, PAs, nurses, and assistants; each level requires a different amount and degree of education. Conversely, each will have its specific reward. Are you willing to sacrifice time with family and endure the long hours and increased stress levels that may come with being a surgeon or practitioner in exchange for financial stability and economic sustainability? As a nurse or assistant, you may achieve the work-life balance you desire, but you may also find that you have to sacrifice your principles of economic stability.

As you define your utopia, each goal and dream will

require you to make a sacrifice. The quicker you understand what you want to be and who you want to be, the easier your life will be.

I was willing to make significant sacrifices to achieve my desired goals.

Ultimately, utopia is a mindset for your life. How can you know if you have achieved something if you have not yet defined it? We know that nothing can be achieved to perfection, but as humans, the best we can do is lay the foundation to get as close as possible, and this begins with defining what that blueprint looks like. It means setting goals for what you want to accomplish and creating a path to achieve them. It is about defining a plan and being prepared for anything that comes your way. It's like a criminal at the door of your home. We often prepare for any attack at our door, but it takes having a plan and a strategy to diffuse any situation. The same is true about everything in life. This is where SPEED comes in.

In the following chapter, I will delve deeper into each of the pillars of SPEED, sharing stories and lessons learned along the way. I hope that by exploring the concept of utopia as a mindset, you will be inspired to define and pursue your version of a meaningful life. After all, utopia isn't just a distant dream; it's a journey we embark on daily.

Quote:

"You can't negotiate with the lion when your head is in its mouth."

~ Winston Churchill

Premises:

- Utopia is a mindset.
- Measure your goals to achieve a successful blueprint, your utopia.
- Achieving perfection is unparalleled.
- Utopia is fluid; your priorities will shift—pivot to meet goals.
- Don't wait until you are 65; nothing will happen without a plan.

Self-reflection questions:

- How do you define utopia?
- How do you achieve utopia?
- What is your developmental barometer?
- What are you willing to sacrifice?

Songs:

- "Good Life" by OneRepublic
- "What's this Life For" by Creed
- "I Lived" by OneRepublic

CHAPTER 2

SPEED

E very Sunday for years, my children and I sat down for our weekly family meeting. Every week, I would ask them what they had accomplished that week and where they went astray. As they got older, I asked them each to create their own acronyms for how they would set their goals and remain accountable to them. Of course, as children do, they grumbled and pushed back. They were comfortable using the framework I had defined for my life in SPEED and were hesitant to develop their own. I was a hardass with them to create, monitor, and hold themselves accountable for progressing in each area. Why? Because, like any parent, I want the best for them, and I know that each of them is destined for success. I needed to make sure they knew how to put themselves on that path.

Each week, if they had not delivered on achieving a goal or had not accomplished what they set out to do, they were then tasked with completing a gap analysis. In other words, where did they fall short and why? Did they have too many commitments to dedicate time to reading their Bible? Did they gorge themselves on junk food or not make time for exercise? What about their schoolwork? The gap analysis is the tool I use to ensure accountability. While some people and businesses evaluate their performance and progress just once per year, it is an integral part of my weekly and daily routine, similar to the developmental barometer.

We often juggle multiple responsibilities, ambitions, and challenges in our fast-paced world. It's easy to become overwhelmed, especially when striving for success while managing personal well-being. Analyzing where we are compared to our goals often becomes secondary to other requirements. For me, it's like breathing—it's ingrained in my being.

The acronym SPEED—Spiritual, Physical, Emotional, Economic, and Development—is a holistic framework to help individuals create pillars for their goals and prioritize their lives effectively. Ultimately, **SPEED is nothing more than a blueprint for a prosperous life**. This concept emerged from my journey of self-discovery, especially after facing the challenges of cancer while raising three young children.

The idea of SPEED came to me late one night when sleep eluded me, and my mind raced. I had achieved a level of professional success and a sense of utopia that many aspire to, yet I felt an acute sense of confusion about what true success truly meant. Despite my financial accomplishments, I realized something essential was missing—a guiding framework to navigate my life's purpose and goals.

As I reflected on my experiences, particularly my battle with cancer, I understood the importance of having a solid foundation in my life. It became clear that true fulfillment lies not just in career achievements but in a balanced approach that nurtures all aspects of our being. Thus, the acronym SPEED became the foundation on which the rest of my life would stand, providing the framework for goal-setting and fulfillment.

S – Spiritual: This aspect encompasses my beliefs, values, and connection to something greater than myself. Nurturing my spirituality has been a source of strength, especially during challenging times. It's about finding peace and purpose, anchoring me in moments of uncertainty.

Being spiritually fit is crucial for me. I identify as a Christian, but my focus transcends religious boundaries. I believe in the necessity of a higher power or a source of strength that can anchor us during turbulent times. Life can be overwhelming, and without a spiritual foundation, the weight of the world can crush our spirits.

Growing up with a rough childhood marked by abuse and instability, I learned early on that human beings cannot absorb the pressures of life alone. When I faced cancer twice, I realized that a spiritual outlet was essential for my resilience. Engaging in practices that nourish the soul is vital to staying spiritually fit. This might include daily readings from sacred texts, meditation, prayer, or reflective journaling. What matters is finding what resonates with you.

P – Physical: This includes my health and fitness. I've learned that caring for my body is vital for longevity and overall well-being. Regular exercise, a balanced diet, and sufficient rest are crucial components that contribute to my sense of vitality.

Our bodies are the vessels through which we experience life, and maintaining physical health is essential for overall well-being. This involves regular exercise and a balanced diet, understanding our bodies' needs, and respecting our limits. If you are not whole or functioning at your physical best, how can you serve others or achieve your goals?

In discussions with my children over a decade of family meetings, I emphasized that being physically fit is not about appearance. The clinical data I have come across consistently shows that physical health is intrinsically linked to mental wellness. When we neglect our physical fitness, we place undue stress on our muscles, tendons, and bones, leading to a myriad of health issues.

Make no mistake, if you are not physically fit, you are more susceptible to major illnesses, such as heart disease and cancer.

I often asked my children, "What did you eat this week? Are you monitoring your diet? Do you understand how certain foods can impact your health?" We discussed cholesterol and blood pressure, reinforcing that being physically strong is vital for resilience against life's challenges. I hope that they never face the massive physical diseases I encountered. Still, I know that if they are not physically strong, they may struggle when confronted with serious health diagnoses.

E – Emotional: Emotional resilience involves understanding and managing my feelings. It's about cultivating self-awareness, practicing mindfulness, and developing healthy coping mechanisms. Emotional well-being has been essential in navigating life's ups and downs, as they are inevitable.

I often ask my children and others, "Are you emotionally and mentally strong?" Since COVID-19, mental health has become a pressing issue in our society. Ironically, I had been teaching my children the importance of emotional strength from an early age.

To foster this, I encouraged them to engage in mentally stimulating activities such as crossword puzzles, chess, and other brain games that would challenge their minds and keep their mental health in check. Being mentally and emotionally strong requires effort and energy, much like physical fitness.

I often remind them to consider how they maintain their mental and emotional well-being. Is it through reading books, watching educational videos, listening to inspirational messages, or podcasts? The question remains: How do you consistently challenge your mind and strike a balance to remain emotionally and mentally strong?

E – Economic: This pillar relates to financial stability and the ability to provide for oneself and loved ones. I've come to appreciate that economic health is essential for reducing stress and enabling opportunities for growth, development, and contributing to my community. My 501 (c) (3) nonprofit would not be nearly as successful in changing people's lives without me being economically sound.

While financial success is not the sole indicator of worth, it provides a practical foundation that allows us to pursue our passions and dreams without the constant stress of financial insecurity.

Being economically savvy involves more than earning a high income; it requires smart budgeting, wise investing, and planning for the future. It's about creating a financial plan that aligns with your values and goals, enabling you to contribute to causes that matter to you.

D – Development: This encompasses personal and professional growth. Continuous learning, setting goals, and seeking new experiences create a sense of fulfillment. It's about striving for progress, no matter how small.

Life is a journey, and we must remain open to new experiences, skills, and knowledge. This can involve formal education, personal hobbies, or professional development. The D in SPEED is an integral part of the premise encompassing all other pillars; give it your all in whatever you set your mind to.

Throughout my life, I've consistently sought opportunities to learn—whether through workshops, reading, or engaging in new projects. Growth requires stepping outside our comfort zones and embracing challenges as opportunities for personal and professional development.

Embracing the SPEED framework has transformed my approach to life. I've gained clarity and a sense of direction by categorizing my goals into five segments: Spiritual, Physical, Emotional, Economic, and Developmental. This holistic perspective not only enriches my life but also allows me to contribute positively to the lives of others.

As you embark on your journey with SPEED, remember that it's not about perfection in each category; instead, it's about striving for balance, fulfillment, and execution. Take the time to reflect on each aspect and how it interconnects. Your path to holistic success awaits, and with the SPEED framework, you can navigate your goals with purpose and intention.

It is important to remember that the emphasis you place on each pillar of your framework will not only look different from mine (therefore, I urge you to create your own), but your priorities will change depending on your stage of life. When I became a father, my priorities shifted; when I had cancer, my priorities shifted. As I move forward into this next stage of my life, while the pillars are the same, the weight of each bucket carries different values. Again, I've had numerous conversations and mentoring discussions with people in all stages of life. And many have asked if they can use SPEED. Some have decided to use the acronym SPEED, while others have created their own acronym to define utopia.

The idea is that, however you have defined your utopia and the pillars that will support your journey, the practice or actions moving you forward must be consistent and even habitual. Eventually, **these habits will become part of your DNA**, a natural part of who you are. It would suffice to say that you may even become a new creature as you develop new routines. SPEED is your blueprint/plan of attack for how you will achieve your goals.

Unfortunately, goal setting is not something that everyone does. I've made lists of my goals since I was twenty years old, and it is just part of who I am. I've asked many young people, recent college graduates, and young professionals about their goals, and I was shocked to learn that many, if not most, had not set any goals for their lives. They may have established the goal to go to college, graduate, and then get a "good" job.

But then what?

Had they even defined what their lives would look like once they had that piece of paper?

Was graduating the ultimate accomplishment?

Of course not! As anyone knows, starting a career, whether college-educated or not, is merely just the beginning and, frankly, a means to an end. Everyone needs to work (even if you don't financially need to) to achieve some other area of fulfillment in your life. Let me give you an example. As I've shared, economic fitness was always heavily weighted as I created the blueprint for my life. The goal was not to worry about money, and to achieve that, I had to make a lot of it.

The question became, how? I would not be satisfied with a career that led me to live an ordinary life. I knew what my utopia looked like, and the premises on which it would be created, in part, revolved around being wealthy. So, I set my sights high.

Conversely, my daughter Libby, who is very in tune with her utopia and has spent time building her framework, does not weigh wealth like I do. She places greater value on sharing the Word of God (spiritual fitness) with the world. Although Libby weighs her pillars differently than I do, make no mistake: She is extraordinary.

As I've mentioned, I hammered the concept of establishing goals into my children, beginning when they were very young, through our family meetings. Yet that does not mean they share the same utopia, have set the same goals, or place the same priorities on the pillars of their lives. One child may save one hundred dollars per week, another may spend that much. They evaluate their lives through similar lenses, but how they apply the structure to their lives differs.

Each of my children have created goals they want to achieve with the ultimate destination of achieving their vision for their lives. I don't expect their paths to be the same as mine; I just want to make sure they have a path to follow rather than allowing life to carry them along the way. The same is true for you, and the reason behind writing this book in the first place. I want you to create the acronym that serves you, gives you the foundation to build your life, check in on your milestones, and reach your goals.

In other words, what is your plan, and how will you weigh the importance of each area or pillar? How will you make your actions habitual and part of your DNA?

Let's go back to the one time of year when many look at their lives through the lens of "new beginnings." New Year's is typically when people evaluate what they accomplished the previous year and set goals for what they want to do in the new year. In reality, **most people fail after a few weeks, or certainly before the end of February, because their goals did not become habits and were not governed by checks and balances.**

By definition, a habit is something that is regularly practiced and difficult to give up. Do you brush your teeth every day? Yes, why? Of course, it is good for you, and your dentist tells you to do it. But the real question is, do you think about it? Do you have to remind yourself daily, "Don't forget to brush your teeth!" No—it is just part of who you are and what you do.

The actions surrounding the pillars in my life are no

different than brushing my teeth—they are so deeply ingrained in who I am and what I do that I do not even have to think about them. It is never a question of whether I will read my devotions in the morning or whether I will do something that allows me to be physically active. I have created routines around every one of the pillars. How else can anyone expect to accomplish anything without taking small steps and forming daily habits to achieve their goals? No Olympic athlete woke up one morning and said I am going to win a gold medal tomorrow. While they certainly had to see this accomplishment as part of their utopia, it was the plan —the framework of goals, habits, and accountability — that got them there.

It's about creating a cadence of continuous action, moving you one step closer to your goal.

Part of the problem is that many people can't see far into the future. They believe that by changing one thing or implementing one "habit" and doing it a few times, they will see a miraculous transformation in the trajectory of their life. If you go out for a run today, will you run in the NYC Marathon this weekend? Of course not, but running one mile today is just the beginning of the long journey toward being capable of doing it. It requires time, effort, consistency, and accountability.

Sadly, I've witnessed countless people wake up and wonder how they got to this stage of life, regretting not having achieved what they wanted for their lives. I guarantee that none of those people had developed a plan, a set of goals and routines that, by taking one step at a time, would have brought them to their utopia. Instead, they were comfortable in the inertia and simply "wished" for their dreams to be fulfilled without putting in the work to achieve them.

Without a doubt, it takes work! You may know what I'm talking about if you've ever started a workout routine. Maybe being physically fit is a desire that has been on your heart, and every day, you say, "I'll start tomorrow." This is the inertia of being comfortable. Of course, doing the work to become physically fit is challenging, and it is much easier for many people not to do it.

But your utopia includes seeing your legacy play out in front of your eyes as you have grandchildren, and you want to watch them grow and thrive. How will you ensure that it comes to fruition? When it comes to your health, you will not wake up one day and suddenly regain your youthful appearance and healthy body. It requires consistently doing daily things that will transform your physical fitness and ensure your longevity and overall well-being.

When I say "ensure," I want to be clear—physical fitness as a pillar does not mean you will not face any challenges or health issues. Case in point—although I take pride in maintaining a healthy lifestyle, cancer still attacked my body at 29 and again at 50 years old. Is it possible that the cancer was a consequence of my actions? Yes—one could argue that stress was the cause of cancer both times. Yet this was a sacrifice that I made because I wanted to be an economic monster, ensuring my financial security and stability.

Because you have a plan (SPEED) and may be prepared for what you think may come your way, you have no idea what storms life will bring. In the broader context of life, it's not about your intentions; you may intend to lose weight, spend less, save more, or start a nonprofit organization, but your actions will ultimately determine whether you achieve the desired outcome.

Back to your pillar of physical fitness. Let's say you define your utopia and have determined that your plan and, ultimately, your New Year's Resolution is to get healthy by joining the gym. If you are like many people, you may expect instant results, such as washboard abs and toned arms, after just a day or two of weight training. Many people don't realize that it takes baby steps and consistent effort to make any progress. Although a goal of losing 30 pounds may seem impossible at the outset, you will be amazed when, after 6 months, you have achieved that goal and exceeded it.

The same is true for every goal and movement toward utopia. You will not attain financial

security or have one million dollars in the bank without putting that first dollar in and then consistently and routinely adding to that account.

Unfortunately, as humans, we often cannot see what the future holds, or we struggle to do the work, so we give up, sliding back into comfort, waiting for someone to wave a magic wand to make us whole, with our bank accounts intact, and our hearts satisfied. I can assure you that no one is going to do the work for you. Yoda is famously quoted as saying, *"Do or do not. There is no try."* You cannot tell yourself that you are going to "try" to live the life you want or that you will "try" to have a successful career.

There are those who do and those who do not.

Which one will you be?

Do you intend to live out your dreams, or will you plan to do so?

What actions will you take today that can be ingrained in your DNA and will push you inch by inch toward your dreams?

It does not matter at what stage of your life you are reading this. If you have never set goals or had a vision for your life, you might think it is too late to start now, or you don't have enough time to achieve what you want in life. I guarantee you that, although we know life is short, it is never too late, and you can still achieve your utopia; it all depends on the actions you are willing to take.

What will you prioritize?

Will you continue to follow the traditional path you have always been on, or are you willing to change your routine, even make sacrifices, to reach that coveted destination of utopia?

I do not believe in the cliché, "You can't teach an old dog new tricks." If you are breathing —and clearly, you are —you can recalibrate where you want your life to go and how you will get there.

As I've mentioned, your utopia may change with life stages and circumstances, but the priorities around how you define the pillars shouldn't change. It's simply how you weigh them.

Time only moves in one direction. If you are not moving forward with time, you are moving backward. What will you define as your acronym to ensure you continue making progress toward a fulfilling and satisfying life?

Quotes:

"Do or do not. There is no try." ~ Yoda

"People will judge you by your actions, not your intentions."
~ Maya Angelou

Premises:

- SPEED is the blueprint for a happy life.
- It becomes part of your DNA, and it requires accountability.
- New Year's goals fail by February because there are no actionable checks and balances.
- If you are not moving forward, you are moving backward.

Self-reflection questions:

- What goals do you want to accomplish? Do you have a plan for your endeavor?
- I broke my framework into the acronym SPEED. What will your acronym be?
- How will you hold yourself accountable?

Resources:

- *The Wealthy Barber* by David Chilton
- *The Millionaire Next Door* by Thomas J. Stanley
- Better You is Better Living by Dan Martell

Song:

- "Let's Go" by Calvin Harris

CHAPTER 3

Ordinary Becoming Extraordinary

It was a Thursday in September 1992, a day that began like any other in College Station, Texas. But for me, it marked the beginning of a profound transformation. For two years, I had drifted through junior college, indulging in the carefree lifestyle of a bar hopper, oblivious to the future that awaited me. The allure of fraternity life had overshadowed my academic responsibilities, and now, the consequences of my choices had come crashing down.

That morning, as I opened the door to my father, the weight of his disappointment was palpable. "Load your stuff," he commanded, his voice steady but filled with an emotion I could hardly bear. My mother's tear-streaked face loomed behind him as she softly urged me to comply, promising to pray over my troubled life. I felt the churning mix of regret and anger as I packed my belongings into the back of the U-Haul, each item a reminder of my failures.

Upon arriving home, the familiar scent of my mother's spaghetti filled the air—her comfort meal for uncomfortable situations. Sitting together at the table, my mother offered a lengthy prayer, asking for grace and forgiveness. I sat across from my father, my heart heavy as I awkwardly pushed spaghetti around my plate, reeking of alcohol and shame. When he declared, "I can't even sit here and eat with you," and left the table, I felt the full weight of my choices settle over me like a shroud.

A few days later, my father drove me in his unmarked police car, a silent testament to the authority he wielded. As we drove in uncomfortable silence, I felt my future slipping through my fingers. After 25 minutes, we reached Bear Creek Park, a sprawling 2,154.6-acre park that soon became my new reality. My father pointed to a small shack and told me I would report there on Monday at 6:00 AM.

He explained how he had worked extra jobs for two decades, averaging over 20 hours a day, to save up for my tuition while juggling night shifts. "I'm just trying to cut my financial losses while saving a son," he said, his voice heavy with unspoken hopes. I stood there, realizing how much he had sacrificed for me, and the gravity of my wasted potential weighed heavily on my heart.

On my first day at Bear Creek, a man approached me wearing worn blue jeans and muddy work boots, his mouth full of tobacco chew. With a big smile, he asked if I was Scroggins and, upon my confirmation, launched into a series of commands: "See that 5-gallon tank of gas? See that weed eater? See those weeds? Get to weed eating." My heart sank. This was my introduction to the world of hard labor, a stark contrast to the life I had imagined.

That weed-eater became my constant companion over the next two years. I learned the ins and outs of Bear Creek, becoming known as the college dropout who had embraced an ordinary life. While my peers envisioned futures filled with potential, I stared into the abyss of a stagnant routine, a county lifer hoping to be promoted to foreman like the others.

Was this the life that was planned for me? Is this how I envisioned the next five, ten, twenty years of my life?

As I reported to work day after day, I began to understand how easy it was to fall into a funk—a cycle of living paycheck to paycheck, conforming to a life of dull contentment—a level of comfort that made me feel frankly self-conscious. I witnessed my coworkers, many of whom had given up on their dreams, drowning in anxiety and devoid of purpose. I realized they had become trapped in the rat race, a cycle from which most never escape.

Standing there, feeling the vibration of the weed eater in my hands, I experienced a **wake-up call**; I was determined not to be one of them. As I matured and learned the ropes, I transitioned from using a weed eater to operating a garbage truck and eventually to the road crew, where I added tractor maneuvers to my skill set. My final promotion with the County left me responsible for managing the park over the weekends.

My mind ran: Is this what I'm going to be?

Was this going to be my life, my destiny?

My life's purpose?

I had kept my college aspirations alive by taking night classes at the University of Houston, leaving my day job in worn-out blue jeans and a dirty work shirt, smelling like yesterday with a stench of oil and gas.

Some people strive for the comfort of an ordinary life, but although I may not be special, I am anything but ordinary. I did not want to be a statistic, a number in the long line of ordinary people—I wanted to be extraordinary. For me, this experience was life-changing and, frankly, a stepping stone that would propel me to set what some may call unachievable goals. I have proven them all wrong.

Why?

Because I knew I could do more, it took me becoming uncomfortable to make a move. I did not enjoy just getting by or the status quo. I witnessed so many others simply accept what they had or make excuses for why they could not achieve more. I watched as others around me content living without fully understanding why they were put on this earth or where they were headed. I like to refer to these people as **"Yeah...buts..."** Problem-solving can be challenging and often requires extra energy and effort; these individuals allow the "buts" to hold them back from taking the necessary actions to achieve their goals.

"Yeah...but..." is an unconscious way of saying "no," for many people, this simple phrase prevents them from taking action, living in their purpose, and achieving their goals. It could even be a limiting belief telling them they are not worthy or deserving, or that they cannot break the stereotype. They allow the beliefs and perspectives of others to govern the level of extraordinary they will achieve. **What is the "yeah...but..."** that has been preventing you from transitioning from ordinary to extraordinary?

The ordinary are typically those people who haven't set a high bar for themselves. They underestimate their capabilities, not believing that they can be or do more because of limiting beliefs, abuse, or negativity they experienced as a child.

Before Roger Bannister broke the four-minute mile in 1954, it was commonly held that running a mile in under four minutes was physically impossible for humans. This belief stated that the human body could not achieve such a feat.

Why was this benchmark established, limiting human potential? Medical professionals and experts wanted to believe it might be possible, but who was willing to defy the odds, push the limits, and test this theory?

Who would be willing to step outside the realm of the ordinary? When Roger broke the four-minute mile at Oxford University on May 6th, 1954, he completely redefined the previously conceived human physical limitations.

Working at the County park was my **wake-up call**. I realized I was wasting my potential, and I was willing to push against the limitations that others had set for me. If I set the bar high enough, I would exceed the limits far above what my mind could comprehend. I could break the analogous 4-minute mile, shattering the box others had chosen to put me in.

When I graduated from college, I faced the same uncertainty many young adults do. I met with a guidance counselor who had never met me, did not know my passions or strengths, and after a brief test, suggested I become an underwriter—a financial analyst for insurance companies.

Needing to get out of my parent's house, I accepted the job, believing it was the right path. However, as I went through training, I quickly realized I was not an introvert. I needed interaction, connection, and the excitement of meeting clients, not sitting in an office crunching numbers. This realization solidified that I could not simply accept that I needed to change something ("yeah…"), and I certainly could not rely on excuses or someone else's perspective of me ("but…") to help me define my life's purpose or direction.

This moment was pivotal. I had initially let someone else define my career path. Where would I be today if I had allowed that definition to limit me? Instead, I challenged myself and transitioned into a consulting role that better fit my mindset, DNA, and utopia.

So, what makes my dreams or motivations any different than yours? Nothing…I chose to take action, flipping the switch on SPEED and being willing to consistently challenge myself to take advantage of every minute of life. I decided to **unlock the potential** that had always been inside me.

Are you willing to become uncomfortable to achieve what you want in life? What does that look like for you? How much energy will you expend/sacrifice to achieve what is extraordinary for you? **What will your wake-up call be?**

Why do you think less than 2% of the population runs a marathon?

Why is it that less than 1% of the authors have become published authors?

And only about 17% of the United States' population makes more than $100K a year?

Why?

Because someone told them they can't do it, or that is all they deserve. And they believe it! Millions of people walk around believing they have to accept their current situation in life, that they only deserve what they have right now. They are unwilling to take action to break free from the ordinary to become extraordinary.

Why?

Because no one has told them otherwise! I am here to tell you that you can and will achieve your utopia.

Now, while your extraordinary may look very different from mine, you do need to define it. My brothers are amazing fathers, husbands, and human beings who have achieved the extraordinary.

Were they millionaires by age thirty? No.

Do they have a non-profit? No.

Have they had to face a major disease? No, thank the Lord!

Does that make them less than extraordinary or even ordinary? No!

Like me, they were able to break free from the stereotypical blue-collar environment that threatened to hold them back. They developed themselves, their careers, and their families; I am so proud of them.

But have they achieved the same level of success in each SPEED premise?

I would certainly say they have not, but how each person defines their pillars and goals, and therefore, utopia, is different. I believe that everyone has the power within them to achieve whatever it is they desire and set their mind to—they just have to unleash it!

Some people are completely fine with the ordinary, and there is a place for them, too. They're solid citizens, and that's okay. Not everyone has it in them, was born to be extraordinary, or wants to make the sacrifices necessary to achieve it, because the **sacrifices will be great**. But if you are reading this book, I am willing to bet that you are *not* okay with being ordinary, willing to accept the status quo, or be content with the path chosen for you.

I chose to take action to lay the foundation on which my future would be created. I was uncomfortable being a statistic and wanted to walk in my purpose. More importantly, I was willing to make sacrifices and pay the piper.

Inertia can be comforting. It offers a false sense of security, a predetermined path with familiar obstacles. However, this comfort comes at a cost. When we allow our lives to be defined by others—by job titles, societal norms, or even familial expectations—we risk losing touch with our maximum potential and ultimately risking our utopia. It is not merely about taking responsibility for our actions but about becoming tactical and using every minute, every second of the day.

Every Minute Counts

Whether it is fair or not, certain individuals will have to work harder than others to achieve extraordinary things due to external pressures and labeling. They will have to ensure that they use every minute more efficiently to achieve the same level of success or to accomplish the same goals.

As I transitioned from ordinary to extraordinary, I faced numerous obstacles and external pressures. Growing up in Tower Oaks Plaza, I was one of the few subdivisions of blue-grey collar households included in the Cypress Creek High School. The majority of the population came from wealthy families. I was not going to allow those external pressures to define me, so I had to apply additional effort and energy, taking advantage of every minute to achieve the extraordinary. I had ADHD, I came from an average neighborhood, my dad was a cop, my mom was a bus driver. I had to go above and beyond with everything I did to even be on a level playing field with those people.

In the world's eyes, I was already framed in a certain light due to how I was raised, where I lived, and our social status. Although those teachers had labeled me based on their expectations of me, I did not allow them to become my limiting beliefs or define me. I would not allow their perspectives to shape or restrict my potential. I was going to be the only one to have control over my destiny. Thankfully, I encountered a coach in high school who recognized my potential and channeled my energy into sports like baseball and football. Those experiences taught me to redefine my identity and embrace my strengths rather than succumb to labels.

If I had allowed others' perceptions and outside pressures to define me, I would have missed out on countless opportunities. The chaos I experienced at a young age, which sometimes caused harm, was not meant to deter me from achieving my goals; rather, it was an opportunity.

The Chinese word "weiji" means both chaos and opportunity. There is opportunity in every challenge, and I certainly took every opportunity I could, building upon the foundation and utopia I had defined for myself.

Life will present us with warning signs at every step of the way. But we cannot let life pass us by; otherwise, we will wake up at 50, 60, or 70 and realize we are not where we want to be. As the song "Warning" by Incubus reminds me, you will raise your head one day and see that you have not achieved what you wanted or desired because you let life happen to you. Warning..."Don't ever let life pass you by."

Why do so many people allow life to happen to them rather than making life happen?

Are they not acting like the extraordinary human beings they were created to be?

Are they allowing fear or others' expectations to hold them back?

A storm may prevent them from achieving, keeping them stuck in the ordinary and taking the easy way out as a **'Yeah, but.'**

In 2000, I experienced a major life event. I was thirty years old, had just left a job making substantial dollars, and had taken a considerable risk on another position with substantial upside.

Without getting too gory, one of my testicles had swollen up. I thought it was a byproduct of my triathlon and adventure races. I stopped at MD Anderson Health Center, and within 2 hours, I was told I had testicular cancer that had spread into my lungs. I asked the doctor if I could continue with my normal day and proceed to my next appointment. His words were "absolutely not." We're admitting you to the hospital. You need to have surgery immediately, and you're likely going to have to undergo radiation and chemotherapy."

At that moment, things flashed through my mind; I had a new job and three young children, and I did not realize where my life was headed. This later hammered home a premise of mine—there are 24 hours, 1,440 minutes, or 86,400 seconds in a day, and I had to utilize every one to overcome this hit of adversity. You will hear other stories throughout this book that capture the premise that every minute counts. Like when I was a child and diagnosed with different disorders, having cancer for the first time burned into my brain that I must utilize every second and every minute to achieve the extraordinary.

I wake up every day of the week and ask myself, "How am I going to allocate every second, minute, and hour to ensure that I stay extraordinary and on the path to achieving my utopia through SPEED?"

The burning idea behind my story is simple yet profound: **Don't let anything or anyone define you**. The world will try to label you—a student, a professional, a parent—but these titles are limiting. They can confine you to a box that doesn't fully capture your essence. Acknowledge the external pressures and expectations, but don't let them dictate your worth or happiness.

The Wolf and the Sheep

As we dive deeper into the journey of self-discovery and purpose, it's important to explore the dynamics of our choices and their consequences. I want to introduce an analogy that has resonated deeply with me: the contrast between the wolf and the sheep. This analogy provides a powerful framework for understanding the forces that shape our lives and the importance of accountability in navigating them, especially as we transition from ordinary to extraordinary. Again, this book is not for the faint of heart, and this analogy may come across as callous. But the fact of the matter is that there are wolves and there are sheep.

Imagine for a moment the wolf—proud, independent, and driven by instinct. It hunts, it thrives, and it adapts. Now, consider the sheep—gentle, often reliant on the herd for safety and direction. While both animals exist in the same world, their approaches to life are vastly different. The wolf embodies the spirit of self-determination, while the sheep often represents complacency and conformity. When I was diagnosed with cancer at age 30, I had a choice: to follow the ordinary and become depressed and deflated, or to continue down the path I had already set out on to become extraordinary. I chose to become a wolf and attacked it.

In our lives, we often face a choice: Do we act like the wolf, taking charge of our destiny, or do we settle into the role of the sheep, allowing external forces to dictate our path? This choice is exacerbated by what I call the "comfort of inertia"—the tendency to remain in our current state, whether that state is fulfilling or not.

It's easy to drift along, guided by the currents of societal expectations or the opinions of others. As you know, from my five years and two months at Bear Creek Park, I experienced a wake-up call that shook me from the inertia that I had spent so long in. Once I realized that I did not want to be comfortable, or more importantly, ordinary, I was determined to change my life forever by becoming the wolf and challenging the status quo.

So, are you a wolf or a sheep? If you watch Denzel Washington movies, then you know where that phrase comes from. I'm not saying to be rogue, disrespectful, or unprofessional, but you must consistently challenge yourself around what and who defines you. There will be people in this world who will not understand you and your value. They may not grasp what you bring to the table, but make sure you know what *you* bring to this world.

Young adults often fear the unknown, feeling paralyzed by the weight of decision-making. I remind them that every choice they make, no matter how small, carries the potential for growth and self-discovery. When people try to put you in a bucket or define your life, I often say, "You must be the one to define who you are."

As you navigate your journey, I encourage you to **consistently challenge yourself** on what and who you should be. Do not let the opinions of others box you in. Embrace the wolf within you—the part of you that is fierce, adaptable, and unafraid to carve your path.

Whether you find yourself in a position of comfort or challenge, remember that inertia can be overcome. Define your identity, resist the urge to conform to societal labels, and recognize that you alone hold the power to shape your destiny.

You *are* the governor of your utopia. As you embark on this journey, let the wolf guide you, and never forget you are the author of your own story.

Quotes:

"It's never too late to be what you might have been."
~ George Elliott

"What lies behind you and what lies in front of you pales in comparison to what lies within you."
~ Ralph Waldo Emerson

Premises:

- What will be your wake-up call?
- To achieve anything valuable in life, there will be sacrifices.
- "Yeah...but..." is an unconscious way of saying "no." Don't limit your potential.
- Don't let anything or anyone define you.
- Consistently challenge yourself.

Self-reflection questions:

- Are you consistently challenging yourself?
- What benchmarks will you use to gauge if you have become extraordinary?
- What are you sacrificing today for a better tomorrow to get you closer to utopia?
- Are you allowing life to carry you along, or are you willing to take control to become extraordinary?

- Are you a wolf or a sheep?

Songs:

- "Forty Six & 2" by Tool
- "Warning" by Incubus

CHAPTER 4

The Storm

Have you experienced the loss of a friend at a young age? Perhaps you've faced the heartbreak of losing a parent or sibling. Have you been diagnosed with a serious medical condition or lost loved ones to a health crisis? Or maybe you've endured the pain of losing someone to the devastation of war? The list of possible catastrophic events that can happen to us in life is infinite, but it is how you overcome these storms that matters.

Each of us will face adversity at some point—whether it's growing up in a divorced home, navigating the challenges of low income, or dealing with the complexities of a single-parent household burdened by addiction or imprisonment. Some may endure the profound loss of a loved one, while others might confront the harsh realities of substance abuse in their formative years.

The reality is that **storms are inevitable.** They rage through our existence, tossing us about like leaves in the wind.

But what is a storm?

A storm symbolizes life's challenges or struggles, varying in intensity and impact for each person. Just as storms differ in size and severity, every individual has their own internal barometer—a unique way of measuring and perceiving the magnitude of their hardships based on personal experiences, resilience, and emotional capacity. What may seem like a mild breeze to one person could feel like a hurricane to another, highlighting the deeply personal nature of adversity.

As I mentor young adults emerging from high school, I often reflect on the storms they've weathered. Many carry heavy burdens that threaten to define them, to trap them in a narrative of victimhood. They may say to themselves, "This is why I can't succeed." But this chapter is a call to arms, a reminder that while adversity is a part of life, it does not have to shape your identity.

Don't get me wrong—it is often easier to blame others and allow life to keep you ordinary than to face our storms and deal with them for what they are. While undergoing chemo, I was given some profound advice as I wrestled with why this particular storm had come my way: **"Live within the question."** There are just some situations that have no answers. There is no one to blame, no particular reason why, and understanding it may be impossible. Instead of allowing it to define you, make you the victim, or derail you from achieving utopia, we must simply learn to live within the question. But that still doesn't mean we should allow it to define who we are.

Let me tell you a story about a young man I adopted who allowed adversity to define him and steal his utopia. Bob was a teenager when he watched his father commit suicide. He continued to live with his mother in a trailer park, where they struggled to survive on very little money. He was 6'4" and 190 pounds of pure athlete. As a star of the football team, he ran a

4.40 and was being considered by all the top universities during his junior and senior years of high school. Bob had all the ingredients to get a full ride to pay for his education—if he weren't trapped in a narrative of victimhood!

Even though he had the physical ability and talent to succeed, he was burdened by the storm he had been through, allowing it to define him rather than taking responsibility for his negative thoughts. He regularly told anyone who would listen, including his football coaches, "You'll never understand what I've been through. You can't imagine how I feel." He played the victim card so often, using it as an excuse for not going to practice or class, that eventually, the coaches had enough and let him go. They compared him to other players who showed up daily to work hard without the excuses of not sleeping well, having a headache, or having a nightmare.

Now he's a security guard, although he had the right circumstances to put him in a better position, breaking the stereotype of where he had come from and what life had handed him. In Bob's case, his storm made him weaker, so his utopia will be even harder to achieve. His storm has defined his identity, and he is letting it hold him back.

Then there is the example of Michael Evans, wide receiver for the Tampa Bay Buccaneers, who was in the home when his maternal uncle killed his abusive father.. Yet, he did not allow this adversity to hold him back from rising to the ranks of an NFL star.

The truth is that adversity can be a powerful teacher. It can refine us, much like fire purifies gold. I have faced my storms—

diagnosed with cancer at 29 and then again at age 50 during the chaos of COVID-19. When I walked into MD Anderson for the first time at age 29, expecting to go to another appointment but was instead told I had to cancel everything, essentially putting my life on hold for six months, I could have seen myself as a victim. It would have been easy to succumb to despair, to wear the label of the victim like a badge of honor. But rather than letting these experiences define me, I confronted them head-on.

Make no mistake; so long as you are breathing, storms will come, so I urge you to do the same—attack them head-on, much like the wolf we talked about previously. Acknowledge the storm, but don't let it become your identity. Life is about choices. You can choose to rise above the chaos or let it pull you under. You should identify your weaknesses and areas where you might need extra effort, but don't stop there. You must keep pushing forward through the storm.

This reminds me of an analogy about the buffalo. When a buffalo senses a storm, it charges directly into it rather than running away, a behavior unique to the animal kingdom. This strategic approach allows the buffalo to spend less time in the storm and emerge on the other side with fewer consequences.

Conversely, other animals run away from the storm, so they spend more time in the worst of it. Human beings do the same thing. We spend so much time trying to avoid the struggles and challenges, even running in the opposite direction to escape them.

But the buffalo's approach reminds us that facing

challenges head-on can lead to a quicker resolution. The quicker that you address the storm, in other words, the quicker that you agree that it is a storm, the faster you will pass through it. On the other hand, the longer you procrastinate in addressing it, the more difficult the challenge may be. Humans often want to retreat or kick the can down the road to delay or avoid dealing with a problem. If you attack something head-on, just as the wind begins to blow and the rain falls, you can minimize the damage or circumvent the struggle.

When we let things fester, it breaks down our premises, and physically, mentally, and developmentally, we become complacent, even slipping into inertia. Eventually, this will impact our utopia.

The first thing you must do when you see a storm coming is ask yourself, **Is it really a storm?** Most people tend to blow something off and push it aside, denying it is a problem until it is a full-blown hurricane.

For example, perhaps your boss just told you they are cutting your compensation by 20%.

Will you simply sit back and wait until it becomes a financial crisis, or will you tackle it head-on?

Consider inquiring about how to earn it back, or explore other job opportunities.

Will this impact your utopia?

What if a loved one is diagnosed with a sickness?

Will you let it fester, hoping it will resolve itself, or will you do something about it?

How will this impact your utopia?

And while we are never fully prepared for storms as unpredictable as they are, by relying on and remaining grounded in our defined pillars of happiness, we can be better equipped to weather the storm, regardless of what it may be.

Who could have predicted that I would experience cancer—not once, but twice—in a lifetime? While I certainly could not foresee that coming, I had my foundation of utopia as my blueprint to help me navigate these experiences.

So, again, please evaluate early on whether a challenge is a storm. Will it impact your utopia? Will it derail you from your path, or is it just a speed bump that delays your progress?

As a former Navy SEAL and now podcaster says, "You have to fight through the storm and emerge stronger on the other side, viewing it as a test that forges character and resilience." Ultimately, the more storms you face or the more adversity you experience, the more you get to **share your experiences** with others to help them through theirs as well.

That's why I sit with people at MD Anderson who are going through chemotherapy; I've lived it. I've been through the storm and come out on the other side, strengthening me. So, now I have a responsibility to help others navigate the storm they are going through.

Now, just because you identify a situation as a storm or a challenge, it does not guarantee that it will be easy or that you will come out unscathed. And then there is the severity of it. You may need to exert more endurance and energy in the storm, but if you don't have the necessary energy or grounding, it will be a long and arduous journey to overcome the problem.

In other words, if you don't have your acronym (SPEED) and you don't have your utopia defined, you might not **be prepared to handle the storm** at any level. If you are weak in SPEED, a storm will further set you back. SPEED helps you prepare. For most people, if not grounded by their utopia, the storm becomes more difficult, and they become victims.

Don't kid yourself. You will have storms, and the more prepared you are, the more you define your utopia and cadence, the easier it will be to navigate through and emerge better and stronger on the other side.

Many young adults I've mentored often fixate on the negativity surrounding them, allowing their circumstances to dictate their potential. They reference their past and struggles as reasons for not pursuing their dreams. This is nonsense. It's a trap that keeps them tethered to their pain rather than propelling them toward their aspirations.

What you need is a shift in perspective. Choose to see adversity as a stepping stone rather than a stumbling block. Choose to attack the storm head-on with a proactive mindset. Each challenge you face is an opportunity for growth, so why not take decisive action to address it? It is in those moments of struggle that we discover our true strength.

At the end of this chapter, you will see in the resources section that I have mentioned Jocko Willink. He often says that when he faces adversity, he uses the simple word: **good**. He knows that every ounce of adversity will make him stronger.

When you encounter your storm, ask yourself: What can I learn from this? How can this experience empower me? Use adversity as fuel. Let it sharpen your focus and ignite your determination. The most successful individuals are often those who have faced the greatest hardships because they understand the value of resilience.

At times during my mentoring sessions, I must get very stern and bold. My charisma and passion come from a deep well of experience; I have seen adversity on many levels. Trust me when I tell you, it was incredibly hard to overcome many trials, and some took years to navigate. Yet, I knew I could not let a single event, person, or adversity impact what I bring to this world. I refuse to let these challenges diminish my value or the contributions I can make.

If you're reading this and thinking, "Kevin, you don't understand what I've been through," you may be right. I may not know your specific struggles, but I have mentored others who have faced the fiercest adversities imaginable. We all have our battles. The real question is: **Will you let the storm define you?**

Young adults often fear the unknown, feeling paralyzed by the weight of decision-making. I remind them that every choice they make, no matter how small, carries the potential for growth and self-discovery. When people or situations try to put you in a bucket or define your life, "You must be the one to define who you are."

If you allow adversity to label you as a victim, there is no one to blame but yourself for the stagnation that follows. You have the power to decide how to respond to your circumstances. You can let the storm knock you down, or you can rise, stronger and more determined than ever.

Remember—storms are inevitable. But you have the power to rise above them. Do not let your past dictate your future. Embrace it, learn from it, and emerge stronger. Your dreams are waiting on the other side of adversity; don't let anything hold you back from achieving them.

As you move forward, remember this mantra: **"My struggles do not define me; I am defined by how I overcome them."** Let this be your guiding light in the darkest of times. The storm may be fierce, but so is your spirit.

Quotes:

"Live within the question." ~ Rainer Maria Rilke

"You have to fight through the storm and emerge stronger on the other side, viewing it as a test that forges character and resilience."
~ Unknown

"Not all storms come to disrupt your life, some come to clear your path." ~ Paulo Coelho

Premises:

- Make no mistake—a storm is inevitable.
- Your experiences during the storm strengthen others.
- Make sure it's a storm and not a bump in the road. The stronger the foundation, the more manageable the storm.
- Leave the victim mentality behind. Don't allow the storm to define you.

Self-reflection questions:

- Will you let the storm define you?
- Ask yourself: Is this really a storm?
- Are you running through the storm or being chased by it?
- Are you kicking the can down the road and letting it fester into a bigger problem?

Resources:

- Jocko Willink "Good" podcast

Songs:

- "Rescue" by Lauren Daigle
- "Blowing in the Wind" by Bob Dylan
- "The Living Years" by Mike and the Mechanics
- "Daylight" by David Kushner

CHAPTER 5

Fear Is a Liar

Fear is a topic that many shy away from discussing, yet it is something that countless individuals grapple with on a daily basis. It can be a crippling force, especially when it comes to making significant life decisions, such as pursuing a new career path or taking **risks that could lead to growth**. I often find myself speaking to recent high school or college graduates, but the truth is, fear knows no age limit. It creeps into the minds of professionals who have been in their careers for years, causing them to hesitate, to second-guess, and ultimately to remain stagnant.

One of the most important lessons I've learned on my journey is that **fear is a liar**. It distorts reality and convinces us to stay confined within our comfort zones. I've seen many talented individuals get stuck in roles that no longer serve them simply because they were afraid to take a leap of faith. This fear can stem from various sources, including the fear of failure, judgment, or the unknown. But here's the truth: if we allow fear to dictate our choices, we forfeit the chance to discover our true potential.

Let me share a personal story that highlights this struggle. In 2000, I was 29 years old, at the pinnacle of my career with an insurance company. I had worked hard to earn my position, rising to vice president and commanding a compensation package of over $300,000. On paper, I was successful. However, I found myself at a crossroads when I received an offer to switch to a consulting role. The entry-level compensation for this new position was $100,000—a significant drop from my current income—but the potential for growth and the opportunity to work directly with clients, rather than solely negotiating with insurance companies, was incredibly appealing.

When I shared this decision with my father, a dedicated policeman for 35 years, he was understandably taken aback. He struggled to comprehend why I would leave a prestigious position for a role that seemed to offer less. His reaction was rooted in traditional notions of success, often equating high income with high value. However, I recognized that this new role would enable me to make a far greater impact on clients and the community. I couldn't let this opportunity pass me by; I felt compelled to embrace the risk for my professional and personal growth. I could envision the potential, even if others couldn't. Initially, fear of failure held me back, but ultimately, I resolved to set that fear aside and take decisive action.

At that moment, I didn't fully grasp how a professional decision would strengthen me spiritually, physically, economically, and mentally, ultimately transforming me into a mental giant/more resilient individual. Deep down, I knew I had to embrace this risk, so I took the leap and accepted the job and the pay cut. Ultimately, that risk allowed me to handle adversity going forward. Little did I know that one year after taking this position, the mental strength I built would allow me to face this diagnosis head-on.

So many people advised me against taking that job, revealing their inability to recognize my potential. Such opinions often limit our growth and hinder our pursuit of excellence, ultimately impacting our utopia. Humans frequently prove to be a snare, providing knee-jerk judgment and opinions based on their circumstances and comfort level of risk. Relying too heavily on other people's opinions or actions can become a trap, potentially leading to bad decisions or compromising your values. Instead of listening to those who did not see my potential, their judgment ignited the mental fire I had in myself, which, little did I know, was equipping me for what was to come next.

You see, after I made that move, I then had twins and was diagnosed with cancer, all within three years. If I were to achieve utopia, I *had* to rely on my defined pillars of SPEED and become an internal mental giant. I could have allowed my diagnosis and treatment, and this bold professional move, to lead to an epidemic of fear, one that is often difficult to shake. I would argue that fear is in all human beings, and how we channel that fear determines our success in achieving utopia.

Let's look at fear in the animal kingdom. The honey badger, indigenous to Africa and Southeast Asia, is willing to do whatever it takes to reach its goal. It is singularly focused on satisfying its voracious appetite, stopping at nothing, no matter how dirty it gets, how much pain it must endure, or how challenging the circumstances may be. I relate its fierce and fearless nature to the human ability for tenacity, determination, and courage. The honey badger doesn't recognize fear as its goal will always supersede it. Unfortunately, as humans, we allow fear to define us and let it bake into our psyche, where it cultivates worry, shame, and anxiety. We should all become like the honey badger, aware of the challenges yet relentlessly pursuing our objectives, not allowing fear, intimidation, or empty judgment to stop us from reaching our utopia.

In my younger, more reckless days, my friends had dubbed me "the Honey Badger." I was seemingly fearless as I navigated life, embracing whatever came my way. Despite the circumstances, risks, or challenges, I relentlessly pursued my objectives, refusing to let those struggles define or deter me. Understand your value and what you bring to the table. Visualizing the road ahead, seeing miles into the future rather than just a few steps, has helped me to understand and overcome the depths of fear.

The naysayers project their fears and circumstances, potentially holding you back, while your core supporters empower you to break free and elevate your journey.

Even though some people may not realize your potential or see the value in taking a risk, there is also value in sharing your thoughts, ideas, and opportunities with your trusted community. Talk to your friends, family, and mentors; lean on their support and insights. This is what I call crystallized collaboration. **There is wisdom in learned experiences**, so before taking any risk, I encourage you to do the due diligence required, speaking with your nucleus of intelligent people around you before jumping toward a goal or investing in something.

As I've mentioned before, cautioning against listening to others may seem contradictory, but it's crucial to distinguish between the naysayers who fill you with fear and your core supporters. Make no mistake: you must define the minions and the nucleus. The minions will project their fear and circumstances, holding you in chains, versus the nucleus breaking the chains and empowering you in elevating your journey.

When I first transitioned from one company to another, a conversation with a friend who was already a CEO left a lasting impression on me. I kept saying, "If I don't succeed here, I can always go back." His advice resonated with me. "Quit looking in the rearview mirror. **Rip that rearview mirror off.** Don't look back. Because if you do, the "**what-ifs**" will always be in your psyche, and you won't be able to give the current opportunity your full energy. **Stop fearing failure.**" By continuing to look back, I kept giving myself an escape route, allowing fear of the unknown or fear of failure to hold me back from giving this new opportunity **my all**.

When you first contemplate a risk or an opportunity, you will have anxiety, fear, and doubt resonating throughout your body. People often continue to look in the rearview mirror, focusing on the "**what-ifs**."

What if it doesn't work out?

What if I fail?

What if I can't go back?

What if I don't succeed?

The reality is that the what-ifs will strangle you and your future if you allow them to. As I mentioned in a previous chapter, the "**Yeah...but...**" and the what-ifs love to hang out together, crippling you in inertia, suffocating your potential.

This is a crucial lesson: do not dwell on what you leave behind. I encourage you to adopt the mindset of looking forward, not backward. The rearview mirror can only bring doubt and fear. Within five years of switching to another position and taking that risk, I surpassed my former income and doubled it in only two years. I am not saying do not learn from your past. If you ask any historian, they will tell you to predict the future—you must look at the past. I am simply saying, do not give yourself an out. Do not let the past impact your DNA to achieve your utopia. Learn from the past, but never let it define you.

But what if I had failed? The more you fail, the closer you are to success. With each failure or setback, you grow and develop, tapping into your strengths and acknowledging your weaknesses. You must use each failure as a lesson to look forward and as a stepping stone to your utopia.

I am sure you have heard the commonly used phrase "the point of no return." It was first used by the pilots fighting in World War II, protecting our Navy ships. It was originally a technical term in air navigation to describe the point in a flight when an aircraft no longer has enough fuel to return to its starting point. The pilots knew their role and their purpose and were determined to succeed.

However, they were also aware of the risks associated with what they were doing. If they stayed on course and followed the plan, they would eventually reach the "point of no return."

Even if they decided to abandon their mission, they would not have enough fuel to return to base, inevitably crashing into the ocean. With this knowledge, they decided to proceed anyway, directing their energy toward their current assignment. There was no looking in the rearview mirror, wondering what would happen if they had made a different decision, turning back before the point of no return. They had to accept their decision, keep moving forward, and never look back.

For many people, the rearview mirror is daunting. It provides them with a security blanket, but that blanket can also be suffocating, defining them and preventing them from becoming extraordinary. They limit themselves to what they think they're capable of. In the end, **fear is just a liar holding you back**, trying to keep you from reaching your potential. Embrace the uncertainty, take the leap, and remember that the most rewarding experiences are beyond your comfort zone. Do not let fear interrupt your growth. The journey is challenging, but it is also transformative. So, take that risk. Your future self will thank you.

Quotes:

"We suffer more in our imagination than in reality."
~ Seneca

"Fear is only as deep as the mind allows."
~ Japanese proverb

"Our lives are what our thoughts make it."
~ Marcus Aurelius

Premises:

- Fear is a liar holding you back.
- Risk can lead to growth.
- Don't dismiss history or the past, but don't let it define you. Rip that rearview mirror off.
- Define the nucleus - define the minions.

Self-reflection questions:

- When was the last time you took a risk and got out of your comfort zone?
- Are you letting your past or circumstances predict your future?
- What lies/excuses are holding you back from achieving greatness? What are you afraid of?

Songs:

- "Crazy" by Seal
- "Fear Is a Liar" by Zach Williams

CHAPTER 6

Necessary Endings

I n the journey of life, personally and professionally, there comes a time when we must learn the art of letting go. This chapter explores recognizing when people, ideas, or processes no longer serve our best interests, enabling us to adopt a healthier, more fulfilling existence.

The concept of necessary endings is rooted in the principle of self-respect and personal growth. There are individuals and ideas that, while they may have once held significance, no longer contribute positively to our lives. This is where the acronym RAV comes into play: **Respect, Appreciate, Value**. If someone—or something—fails to embody these qualities in your life, it is essential to let them go or manage them to the periphery. Ultimately, **letting go is vital for professional and personal evolution.**

To better understand the dynamics of relationships, I often use the analogy of a deep-rooted tree. Picture your life as a tree, with various components representing the people and ideas surrounding you.

Leaves are the most transient elements of this tree. They appear vibrant and full of life, but are often superficial connections that fall away at the slightest breeze. These individuals are typically drawn to you for their benefit—they may enjoy how you make them feel or the energy you bring into their lives. However, their interest is not rooted in genuine care for your aspirations or well-being. I refer to these individuals as "flesh eaters," as they can drain your energy without offering real support in return. It is crucial to discern who your true friends are, especially for young adults transitioning from college to the professional world. Recognizing that leaves will come and go like the seasons allows for a more resilient mindset. We must not present anger toward them; it is simply their nature to flutter away.

Branches, on the other hand, present a more complex challenge. They appear sturdy and reliable, offering support and companionship. However, when storms arise—whether personal trials or professional setbacks—these branches will break, and they typically have a deeper impact on your heart and soul. Relationships with these individuals can often lead to hurt and disappointment. It requires time and experience to truly gauge their strength. When such events unfold, it becomes clear that these branches, too, must be let go. The process may be painful, but it is vital to personal evolution.

At the core of our tree lie the roots—the steadfast individuals who provide unwavering support and nourishment. The roots are the foundation. Not many people understand the gravity of a tree: a tree is gravitropic. As a tree grows upward, it also consistently grows downward into the ground. Above ground, you see the beautiful tree with its flowers, leaves, blossoms, and fruit. Below is cold and dark, where the roots provide foundation and support. The roots are your nucleus that remains consistent when cold and dark. If you find four to five roots that secure your foundation, stay strong with them. These are typically family and a couple of close friends.

As my grandfather, one of my best friends, once told me, "Kevin, when you die, most of the people at your funeral are going to be family, and you will have three to four close friends. If you have done this and built a strong nucleus, you have accomplished a material goal in life. Friends come and go, family, and your core nucleus will always be there." I hold on to this premise dearly. **If you look at your circle/nucleus and do not get inspired, then you don't have a circle; you have a cage.**

This principle of letting go and properly tiering relationships becomes even clearer through the story of the scorpion and the frog. The narrative illustrates a fundamental truth about human nature and relationships, applicable in personal and professional contexts.

In this tale, the scorpion and the frog are on the lower bank of the river as the waters begin to rise. The frog stands at the river's edge, preparing to jump to the higher bank to escape the rising waters. A scorpion approaches, ready to sting him. The frog pauses and says, "Hold on a minute! If you sting me, you will die too." The scorpion, momentarily swayed by the frog's logic, reluctantly agrees to ride on his back across the river. However, just as they near the opposite bank, the scorpion, driven by its inherent nature, stings the frog. As they both begin to drown, the frog cries out in despair, "Why did you do that? We were so close to safety!" The scorpion simply replies, **"That's just what I am."**

This story serves as a poignant reminder: as you navigate your life, you will encounter individuals who may inherently act against your best interests. The quicker you identify someone's character, the easier it is to let them go or place them in the appropriate tier within your life. Remember that just because you know *who* they are doesn't mean you know *what* they are. Those who do not respect, appreciate, or value you can often be likened to the scorpion, acting according to their nature, which may ultimately harm you.

Letting go or pruning is not an act of malice; rather, it is an essential process of self-preservation and growth. Pruning means cutting away dead or overgrown branches to increase fruitfulness and growth. Just as a tree needs to be pruned to encourage new growth, we need to mindfully trim away those things and people that are no longer moving us in the right direction so that we, too, can continue to flourish and achieve our utopia. It can be daunting, but ultimately leads to a more authentic life. By understanding the various roles individuals play in our lives, we can make informed decisions about who deserves our time and energy.

The sooner you figure this out, the sooner you understand how close someone should be to your nucleus and at what layers of the periphery they should lie. There will be some who are willing to give you the unadulterated truth. On the other hand, with some people, you will have to filter their message. The quicker you figure out their DNA and what they are made of, the quicker you can prune the branches where necessary to make room for new growth. Pruning is required to ensure that those who do not serve you stay out of your future and block your present. Unfortunately, in your professional life, you may be unable to let go of all those who require it. Instead, you will have to learn to place them in the appropriate tiers within the peripheral.

A personal example of this is when I was coaching my son's Little League Baseball team. We had made it to the Little League World Series, a massive accomplishment for 10 to 12-year-olds. I was proud of these boys for achieving this level of success, arriving at the highest level of competition in the country for youth baseball. While this achievement should bring out the best in kids (and their parents), unfortunately, it brought out many people's true character. I quickly learned about some of the parents and their hidden agendas. To manage the many characters I encountered, I hired a general manager whose sole responsibility was to manage the parents. I couldn't let go of those I felt had their agenda or were less than genuine. I had to understand who they were, what they were, and what I should expect from them.

Most people close to me often say I have too big a heart or give people too many chances, and they are right. This is a weakness I have had to identify with and channel appropriately. Through the process of letting go, I have learned there must be endings with relationships, careers, and friendships If they don't respect, appreciate, and value you; otherwise, they have their own agendas. They will take chunks of flesh, ultimately preventing you from achieving the extraordinary and your utopia.

We often feel guilty about letting go, citing long relationships or inadequate reasons. But I believe that people come into our lives for a specific "reason" (to teach you a lesson, fulfill a need), for a particular "season" (a temporary period of shared growth), or to stay with you for a "lifetime" (a long-lasting, committed relationship), suggesting that not every connection is meant to last forever. Still, each can provide valuable experiences, lessons, and opportunities. Guilt is a peculiar emotion; similar to fear, it can impact your judgment and hinder your future. If you let guilt prohibit the pruning, that will directly correlate to your growth.

We may want to let go of someone closest to us, but we may not be able to, due to the nature of the relationship. We all know (and love) that crazy aunt or meddling cousin. We may be unable to prune away the family member who is constantly negative or places limiting beliefs in our minds. Yet, if we can define who and what they are, we can keep them where they belong in the role they play—they do not have to be in our nucleus.

As I have stated in this book many times, most humans fall into a routine, and the analogy I use is that of a car traveling 70 mph down the highway. They are in the car, safe, following the speed limit, aware of their surroundings, but settled into mediocrity. There is an exit approaching with the sign named Utopia. Exiting would require speeding up, slowing down, and changing lanes, which I correlate to cleaning up your nucleus.

Here is some simple advice: Take the exit. **Be intentional and aware of your nucleus.**

You always want to be sure that you have the right people around you who will not only help you achieve the extraordinary but also support you to stay there. Doing so will sometimes require you to operate with grace and love, knowing that, as humans, people are imperfect. That's the cool thing about life, though, as Robin Williams' character says in *Good Will Hunting*, "...we get to choose who we let into our weird little worlds."

Distractions or misfires, in the form of things or people, can prevent you from becoming extraordinary, directing or allocating your time and energy where they are not needed. Unfortunately, we often bring someone into our nucleus only to discover they are an eminence front, a facade, a distraction that requires pruning—a cage to our freedom. As the ancient proverb states, "**If you walk with a limp, you will soon limp yourself.**"—We become like the people we spend the most time with. Who do you spend the most time with? Are they lifting you or hindering you?

Are you the most intelligent person in the room? You might find yourself in a room in which you have the most experience, knowledge, and wisdom. From whom would you then find inspiration and new knowledge? How could you continue to support and move toward your utopia without growing and learning?

As humans, we constantly mirror one another. There are countless phrases of this fundamental human characteristic: like attracts like, stick with the pack, etc. Yet, if we are attracted to others like ourselves or are just mirroring one another, how are we motivated to do or be more? As successful as I have been in creating the life I want, living out my utopia as I have defined it, I never want to be the smartest or most successful person in the room. If you find yourself in this position, it is time to find a new room. As I've noted, if you walk with a limp, you will soon limp yourself. If you gravitate to the crowd, you could likely get caught up in mediocrity.

Throughout my career and personal life, I have had to prune people and things out of my life if they no longer support my definitions of SPEED and utopia. Although it may have been uncomfortable and sometimes messy, I know that with each letting go, I moved one step closer to the life I wanted.

I have also learned that it is not only okay but often necessary to say No! Saying "no" allows you to prioritize your time and energy, protect your well-being, set boundaries, and focus on what truly matters to you. It also creates space for more fulfilling connections and opportunities, those that better align with your pillars, priorities, and utopia. As humans and leaders, we have a responsibility to respect and love all, with no exceptions. We need to place people in the appropriate layers around the nucleus, keeping the nucleus tight, with aligned energies and expectations, not a cage but a springboard.

The necessity of endings cannot be overstated. Whether in our professional lives or personal relationships, letting go of what no longer serves us is crucial for growth and happiness. Embrace the process, be mindful of your connections, and always remember: to make room for new beginnings, sometimes we must first create necessary endings. Let them go, and in doing so, make space for the life you truly deserve.

Quotes:

"If you are the smartest person in the room, you're in the wrong room." ~ Confucius

"The quality of your relationships determines the quality of your life." ~ Esther Perel

"You are the average of the top five people you spend the most time with." ~ Jim Rohn

"If you walk with a limp, you will soon limp yourself." ~ Proverb

Premises:

- RAV = Respect, Appreciate, Value
- The process of letting go is vital for professional and personal evolution.
- Be intentional and aware of your nucleus. Prune those who are holding you back.
- People are in your life for a reason, a season, or a lifetime.

Self-reflection questions:

- Are you the smartest person in the room?
- Does your nucleus inspire you, or are they a cage, holding you back from your true potential?

- Are you ready to make the tough decisions and prune the people in your life who are negatively impacting your future?

Songs:

- "Eminence Front" by The Who
- "Rebel" by Ann Wilson
- "Sapling" by Foy Vance
- "Free Bird" by Lynryd Skynryd

CHAPTER 7

Dream Big

As I mentioned earlier, Sundays in our household were special. They were reserved for family meetings, a tradition I cherished deeply. During these gatherings, we would discuss the acronym SPEED—a crucial guiding principle in our lives. But beyond that, I introduced the Scroggins' Premises, a collection of life lessons that shaped our character and values. These premises spanned a wide range of topics, from the importance of resilience when storms hit to the virtues of patience—being **slow to speak and quick to listen,** and the necessity of finding the good in one another. I realized that each of these Scroggins' Premises was also an inherent character trait.

Above all, I instilled in my family that resilience and perseverance can overcome any adversity one might face. But no meeting felt complete without my rallying cry: **"Dream Big!"**

In a world bustling with dreamers, I understand that dreams could be both a source of inspiration and a challenge. Many people aspire to achieve greatness, yet few are willing to put in the necessary work, employ effective behavioral tactics, and maintain unwavering energy to make those dreams a reality. It was crucial for me to ensure my children understood this dynamic.

Let me give you an example of children I taught in my early years in the church preschool. I would ask 10 children under the age of five what they wanted to be when they grew up. 90% of the girls would say, "A princess!" I would ask, "How do you get paid to be a princess?" They would reply, "We get paid by dressing up!"

Fifty percent of the boys would say, "A professional athlete or an astronaut." This demonstrates how, when we are young, we have no limit to our imagination and creativity. At such young ages, it's incredible that children have no fear of chasing their dreams, yet many adults fail to continue dreaming as they age. Psychology Today says, "the average 4-year-old laughs 300 times a day. The average 40-year-old? Only four." It seems that around the same time we stopped dreaming, we also stopped laughing.

Growing up, I faced my share of challenges—my childhood was not without its hurdles, and my college years were fraught with difficulties. Yet, I emerged from those experiences with a fierce determination to succeed. I have always dreamed of owning my own company and becoming a millionaire by the age of 30, having a second home, and owning a Ferrari. I have always dreamed of having a revenue stream to aid less fortunate people and going on a mission trip in hostile territory. I also dreamed that my children would never have to pay for their education. I even dreamt of throwing out the first pitch at an Astros game and shooting the first free throw at the Rockets game! Even with the adversity I have faced, I got it all done...I accomplished my dreams. I never stopped dreaming big, and as one dream came to fruition, a new goal post was planted! I wanted my children to know that while the road to success is often rocky, it is also incredibly rewarding.

As we gathered around the table, I could see the spark of ambition in my daughter's eyes. One of her dreams, though she didn't always voice it, was to become valedictorian of her high school. For her, this was no small feat. A's were a challenge throughout high school, requiring significant stress, effort, and an unbelievable level of discipline. Maintaining a position at the top of her class meant consistently scoring not only A's, but she had to do that in the highest-level classes, scoring between 95 and 100 on tests and papers. She was always aware that someone was chasing her, pushing her to excel.

When the final year of high school arrived, Elizabeth achieved her dream—she was named valedictorian. Though not always illuminated in our conversations, this accomplishment was a significant milestone, a dream memorialized through our countless discussions. I was ecstatic; she had accomplished something monumental, a testament to her hard work and dedication. Not only did Elizabeth achieve her dream of being named valedictorian, but she was also a leader outside of high school with various volunteer projects and leadership positions throughout her church community.

As we celebrated that achievement, I knew another important dream lay ahead for her. Elizabeth aspired to find a college where she felt academically challenged and spiritually connected. She received scholarships from almost every college in Texas, including a full ride from the major Division I schools. Yet, she chose to continue dreaming big. Instead of opting for a cost-free education in Texas, she attended Wake Forest University, a school that offered no financial support.

Her choice was not just about prestige but about pursuing a vision that resonated deeply with her. Graduating with honors from Wake Forest was another testament to her commitment to dreaming big, showing her willingness to invest in her future, even without the financial safety net. Elizabeth now works for a consulting firm in Washington, D.C., assisting with the Christian movement.

Dreaming big isn't solely about personal achievements; it's also about using those experiences to impact others. A few years into my career, after surviving cancer for the first time, I recognized a calling to change lives. Inspired by my journey, I co-founded a nonprofit organization with a good friend. It was an organic process; I felt God had instilled in me a spirit of helping others. It was about **changing lives**!

The idea crystallized during a crisis in our community when forest fires ravaged homes and destroyed property. My friend and I acted swiftly, raising funds and establishing our nonprofit. This endeavor was a true homerun—a culmination of small efforts and incremental victories that ultimately led to a significant impact. We named it Santa's Elves (www.santaselvestx.com) with the premise of **always changing lives**, embodying our mission to make a difference. Dreaming big is using those storms, lessons, and experiences to impact others. This is a perfect example as you further define your SPEED acronym. Santa's Elves assist me in my Emotional bucket. Many renowned psychologists have proven that helping others has a profound impact on your emotional and mental stability.

There's a lesson in this journey: As you dream big, you may experience small wins—singles and doubles that contribute to your ultimate goal, the home run. Creating a tactical roadmap and blueprint for achieving those dreams is essential. **There is power in cadence, discipline, and intention**. Be bold about what you want, and take actionable steps toward your aspirations.

Then there was my son Keaton's big dream—baseball. Or so it was at a point in time. When we were coming home from the Little League World Series, where he was MVP, Keaton casually said, "Dad, I'm going to quit baseball, and I only want to play golf." He was already primed for potential baseball scholarships as only a sixth grader. While we lived on a golf course, he would watch me play. He was a decent golfer, and that was the extent of his experience with the sport. He was unconsciously incompetent. He didn't know what he didn't know. But he had a dream! So he started hitting balls (hundreds daily) and began taking lessons. Long story short, he became the number one player of his high school team and conquered the district. Before Keaton was 18, he had his first hole-in-one at Pelican Hill in Newport Beach, CA—no small feat, regardless of age. The lesson here is that if you want to dream big, it will require intense effort.

My other son, Charles's, idea of dreaming big wasn't academic or physical; his revolved around becoming a strong "gamer." He was outstanding at a game called "Fortnite" and rose high within the Fortnite ranks. Instead of using a remote, he invested in a keyboard and a larger screen, making him more efficient and a dominant player. While some would dismiss this as dreaming big, Charlie ultimately grew a significant following, and at one point he had a revenue stream from his gaming efforts! As you can see, while my children's dreams are uniquely their own, each of them is always chasing them!

Elizabeth, Keaton, and Charlie demonstrate that when you set your sights high and dream big, not only will it require tenacity and perseverance, but these traits can also help you achieve them.

It is also important to note that dreams are fluid in nature. Dream big simply means that you have laid out your utopia and have the courage and discipline to pursue it. As I have witnessed with Keaton, no dream is unattainable, even with a quick shift. The question is, regardless of the dream, obstacles and unforeseen circumstances will inevitably present themselves.

Life will try to derail your plans at every turn—getting off course does not mean that your dreams are not achievable— you might need to redirect or recalibrate. If a distraction has you allocating energy toward something other than your dream, redirect, get back on track, and keep moving toward your dream.

To dream big and chase them, you must have some inherent character traits, such as resilience and perseverance. When an inevitable storm hits, you must dig deep to find the character trait that will help you push through to the other side.

The stronger the foundation, the stronger the acronym (SPEED), the easier it is to navigate the storm. If your foundation is strong, the storm will make that dream much more achievable. That also bleeds into the premise of dreaming big. The easier you navigate the storm, the bigger your dreams will become, as it helps you understand and realize that you are a mental giant. Overcoming a storm helps shape your psychology in relation to the magnitude of your dreams.

Once I overcame cancer for the second time, my dreams transformed and magnified. Now I want to walk on the moon and sing the National Anthem on a national forum— I've never sung a day in my life, so this will require me to invest time in singing lessons.

Remember that your fight is not with man; it is with yourself.

Reflecting on those Sunday meetings with my children, I realize they were more than just discussions; they were the foundation of our family's values. I wanted my children to grow up knowing their dreams were valid and their aspirations deserved to be fought for. I wanted them to understand that dreaming big is not simply about lofty goals but cultivating the tenacity to chase those dreams with vigor.

Ultimately, it's not just about achieving success as defined by the world. It's about finding fulfillment in the journey, embracing the challenges, and celebrating the growth that comes with pursuing one's dreams.

As I conclude this chapter, I urge you to dream big, not just for yourself but for those who look up to you. Inspire them, support them, and, most importantly, remind them that the sky is not the limit; it is merely the beginning. And let me be frank: when I was a child, I no doubt wanted to be the next Nolan Ryan or Aaron Rodgers. This is why I say dreams are fluid. Once I realized those dreams were not attainable based on my DNA, I amended them, continued to dream big, and chased them.

Go chase your dreams!

Quotes:

"Dare to dream big, then do something about it!"
~ HD Ryan

"The future belongs to those who believe in the beauty of their dreams." ~ Eleanor Roosevelt

Premises:

- Be slow to speak and quick to listen.
- When you pursue your goals, you change lives.
- There's a lesson in the journey.
- Dreaming big requires cadence, discipline, and being intentional on the journey.

Self-reflection questions:

- What are your dreams?
- What is your plan of attack to achieve your goals and ultimately your utopia?
- What is your cadence of actionable daily steps you will take to move closer to your aspirations, and are you disciplined in your routine?

- What are you willing to sacrifice today for a better tomorrow?

Songs:

- "Amazing Grace" by Alan Jackson
- "The Gambler "by Kenny Rogers
- "Only Shooting Stars Break the Mold" by Smash Mouth
- "Dream On" by Aerosmith
- "Don't Stop Believing" by Journey
- "I just want to celebrate" by Rare Earth

CHAPTER 8

Don't Park Your Brain

In the whirlwind of my early 20s, a time marked by a loaded schedule and relentless ambition, a weekly ritual grounded me—visiting my grandfather. A man of simple pleasures and profound wisdom, he had weathered the Great Depression and emerged with an unshakeable spirit. Each time I rushed in, eager to share my latest career moves, he would say, 'Let's sit down for a minute.' Over cups of coffee or a Coca-Cola, we would exchange words and the very essence of connection. We laughed and relaxed, free from the distractions of technology and modern life, as he imparted wisdom that would shape my understanding of my professional and personal relationships, which would later sustain me.

In a world that often prioritizes hustle over heart, those conversations illuminated a simple truth: We find joy and meaning in our relationships. In those moments, I learned that true fulfillment lies not in our ambitions but in the personal relationships that nurture our souls. When I was spending time with him, I was never worried about the next meeting on my schedule.

At Starbucks, I often observe high school students flooding in for their caffeine fix, their eyes glued to their phones. A glance at one another is quickly followed by a return to their screens, as if disconnecting for even a moment would be unbearable. This pervasive lack of genuine connection concerns me, especially as research shows that human interaction and touch are essential for our well-being. The simple truth is that relationships cannot be built or maintained through technology.

Of course, technology plays a vital role in our lives, but it should never replace the most powerful organ we possess—our brain. The most significant discoveries, including technological advancements and artificial intelligence, sprang from human thought. While I embrace my cell phone for calls and texts, I worry that the constant presence of screens diverts our attention from the people physically around us.

The ripple effects of eliminating human interaction and relationships will be devastating for future generations, creating isolation, mental health issues, misfires, distrust, and missed opportunities for deep connection. The remedy is to develop strong interpersonal communication skills, which will foster strong relationships. It's not about quick texts or smiley face emojis, but about investing 6-8 minutes to hold a meaningful conversation with another human being. This means pausing to put the other person first, being patient, and investing in them. Are you ready to make that effort?

In an age defined by screens and connectivity, I will be bold and say that technology has inhibited the cerebral horsepower of human beings' ability to tap into the full scope of their brains. This isn't just speculation; it's a conclusion drawn from observing my children's screen time and my experience across various companies. While technology brings undeniable efficiency, it often becomes a crutch, preventing us from using our inherent talents. Make no mistake: technology and artificial intelligence will need to be part of your tactical plan—SPEED—to achieve your Utopia, but it cannot replace your cerebral horsepower and your gut.

One of the companies I'm involved with highlights this balance between efficiency and human engagement. In my 30s, we composed our presentation decks for sales meetings to showcase our capabilities in the insurance space. Sure, there were typos and misfires, and the results might not have been aesthetically pleasing, but we created substance that reflected our team's expertise. It was not efficient, but it was authentic.

Fast-forward to today: the company now utilizes standardized presentations that are nothing short of magnificent. With a few clicks on the keyboard, you can quickly check capabilities, perform gap analysis, and deliver strong, polished presentations. While this technological advancement has propelled the company forward, it raises critical questions: Have the individuals who use these tools truly engaged with the content? Are they merely checking boxes and printing presentations without understanding their substance?

For reference, a February 2025 Forbes article titled 'AI Is Making You Dumber' highlights a recent study by Microsoft and Carnegie Mellon University that raises concerns about AI's impact on our cognitive abilities. Researchers found that workers increasingly relying on AI reported diminished critical thinking skills as their focus shifted from independent problem-solving to merely verifying and integrating information. This phenomenon suggests that, much like a muscle, the brain requires regular exercise to maintain its strength; without routine practice of critical thinking, cognitive faculties risk atrophy. The irony lies in the fact that while AI can improve efficiency, it also deprives users of essential opportunities to engage their judgment, leading to a narrow-minded approach to problem-solving. As we become increasingly dependent on AI tools, we may lose our ability to think critically and mistakenly believe that our intellectual capabilities are waning. The implications of this overreliance could be profound, urging us to strike a balance between AI integration and the need to nurture our cognitive skills.

I would never call technology the enemy, but it is slowly numbing us, impacting mental health, relationships, and limiting cerebral horsepower, which ALL bleed into becoming extraordinary, dreaming big, and maximizing utopia, ultimately hurting the innovativeness and creativity of the next Albert Einstein. This is what I mean by urging us to find a balance. Technology can enhance our efficiency, but we must also engage our cerebral horsepower to comprehend and appreciate the work we build and present fully.

For many, cell phones are a normal part of life, a universal presence woven into the fabric of daily existence. But let's take a moment to remember that there was a time when our communication needs were met without the constant glow of a smartphone. Just thirty years ago, cell phones were a novelty. Before their rise, we relied on landlines and payphones. Now, we enjoy instant communication and global connectivity, but we also face significant drawbacks, decreased face-to-face interaction, digital addiction, and privacy concerns.

Today, the average person checks their phone every twelve minutes, accumulating to a staggering 120 times per day. 44% of adults in the U.S. report experiencing anxiety when separated from their devices. It's time for a collective moment of self-reflection. How often do we find ourselves mindlessly scrolling, our brains effectively parked while our fingers do the walking?

Just as we welcomed the advancements of cars, microwaves, and washing machines, there's nothing inherently wrong with technology making our lives more efficient. However, we now find ourselves at a crossroads where that efficiency has begun to encroach on the most fundamental aspects of our lives: our relationships. Technology allows us to park our brains, rendering them numb to the richness of human connection.

The pandemic forced an unprecedented shift toward remote work, with business conducted primarily over the phone or through platforms like Webex. This drastic change led to a significant reduction in human interaction. Mental health claims in America surged, with reports indicating a 30-40% increase in prescription drug use for anxiety and depression. Countless studies reveal the detrimental effects of isolation; individuals who were cut off from the world experienced a dramatic decline in mental resilience.

I'm not here to judge. I understand that mental illness is real; I have experienced its heavy weight myself. But I am compelled to emphasize that we cannot afford to park our brains. We cannot rely on technology to fulfill the innate human need to connect. Our phones are not a substitute for genuine, meaningful relationships. We cannot allow artificial intelligence to overshadow our ability to engage our brains, hearts, souls, tongues, and mouths in fostering connections that bolster mental strength.

As artificial intelligence becomes more integrated into our lives, it increasingly influences how we express ourselves, often leading to a loss of authenticity. Recently, I found myself navigating the dating scene at 53, feeling good about a connection with a woman. I was genuinely excited when I received a text from her that seemed heartfelt and thoughtful. After sharing my excitement with my daughter, she quickly pointed out that the message was probably a product of AI, lacking the real emotional depth that comes from a genuine connection. When the girl I was dating confessed that she used AI to craft it, I felt a wave of embarrassment and disappointment wash over me. While I was fine with technology helping us connect initially, using it for something so personal felt like a betrayal.

The experience made it clear that relying on AI for emotional expression can create a façade of connection while eroding what it means to be human. I was left grappling with a disconnect—not just with her, but with my authentic self. In a world where meaningful communication is increasingly filtered through algorithms, I can't help but wonder how many others are caught in the same struggle, torn between the convenience of technology and the desire for genuine connection.

As we navigate this tech landscape, it's crucial to recognize the power of human interaction. Conversations, laughter, and shared experiences are vital to our emotional well-being. They stimulate our brains, ignite our creativity, and reinforce our resilience. When we lean too heavily on technology, we risk missing out on the joys and challenges of engaging with others.

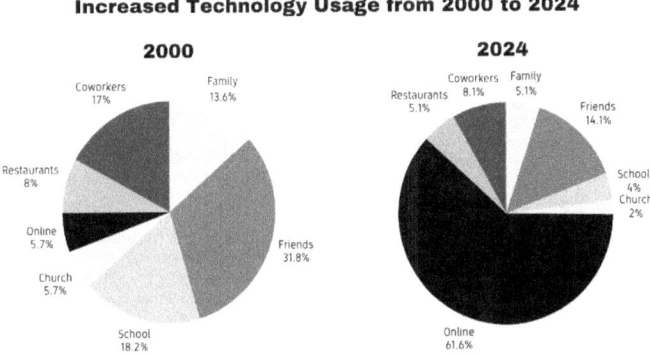

The above graph illustrates how people spend their time, which has undergone drastic changes since the invention of the computer. This shift has raised significant concerns about a growing disconnect from what truly matters in life. Once characterized by shared meals and outdoor activities, family time is being replaced with quiet dinners in front of glowing screens and children choosing gaming devices over throwing the ball outside with their fathers. While friendships have expanded through social media, the depth of their relationships often pales in comparison to the warmth of in-person gatherings, leading to a sense of isolation even among those who are technically 'connected.'

In the workplace, the rise of remote work, while offering flexibility, has blurred the lines between personal and professional life, often resulting in burnout and a lack of camaraderie among colleagues. Schools have adapted to different forms of digital learning. Still, the absence of physical classrooms can diminish the richness of social interactions and collaborative learning experiences that foster genuine connections and further advancements. Even church attendance has migrated to some extent online, with virtual services replacing the communal spirit of worship, leaving many longing for the sense of belonging that physical presence provides.

Entertainment has even shifted from communal activities like movie nights to solitary streaming. These are all examples of cultural issues that technology is driving. As it pervades our lives, there is a palpable loss of humanity, empathy, and authentic connection. The convenience of digital interactions cannot replace the profound emotional and social benefits of in-person relationships, highlighting an urgent need to reevaluate our priorities and reconnect with the essence of what it means to be human in an increasingly virtual world.

In this era of screens and devices, let us strive to reclaim our cognitive abilities. Instead of parking our brains, let us put them to work. Engage in discussions that challenge our perspectives, share experiences that enrich our lives, and foster relationships that bring fulfillment. The richness of life lies not in the efficiency of our technology but in the depth of our connection to one another.

Next time you reach for your phone, pause for a moment. Consider the power of conversation, the warmth of a friendly smile, or the simple joy of being with someone you care about. Make a conscious choice to be present. After all, in a world increasingly dominated by technology, the most powerful tool we have at our disposal is our ability to connect.

Quotes:

"Great minds discuss ideas; average minds discuss events. Small minds discuss people." ~ Eleanor Roosevelt

"The quieter you become, the more you are able to hear." ~ Rumi

"People won't remember what you said; they'll remember how you made them feel." ~ Maya Angelou

Premises:

- Don't allow technology to eliminate authentic human interactions. The simple truth is that relationships cannot be built or maintained through technology.
- AI will limit your cerebral horsepower if you abuse it. While technology brings undeniable efficiency, it often becomes a crutch, preventing us from using or losing our inherent talents. Find the balance.
- Hold meaningful conversations. Pause, have patience, and invest in your relationships.

Self-reflection questions:

- Are you over-relying on AI?
- How often are you picking up your phone throughout the day?
- Do you have more conversations through technology than in person?
- Are you willing to invest in your relationships by prioritizing the other person to foster deeper connections?

Songs:

- "We Are Young" by Fun
- "Should Have Seen It In Color" by Jamey Johnson
- "Walk" by Pantera

CHAPTER 9

WAR

W hen I was in fourth grade, I struggled a lot in class. Mr. Palmquist, the principal at the private school I attended, called my dad, who was in Special Operations, "Lieutenant Scroggins, Kevin is having a hard time again. Do I have permission to discipline him?" My dad gave him the green light, and I remember dropping to my knees and praying to Jesus. Then came the discipline—the desk, the consequences—the swat, that happened probably 100 times a year. This was a private school where I was forced to attend because I was diagnosed as hyperactive with attention deficit.

Eventually, I found an outlet. My dad refused to put me on ADHD medication, so when I got to junior high and high school, I turned to athletics instead. All the energy, all the distractions—I channeled them into sports. And it worked. I became a strong athlete, even a standout. Instead of being sent to the principal's office, I started getting sent to the coach's office, where they'd run me or make me do calisthenics.

Through that experience, I became deeply aware of my weaknesses. But "weakness" is a tricky word. Who defines what our weaknesses are? Only you can decide, using the developmental barometer I mentioned earlier. For some people, it might be impatience or arrogance, procrastination, or a lack of confidence. My weaknesses were more clinical.

ADHD and OCD made focus difficult, but they also came with strengths, like a high intellectual capacity. The key wasn't to ignore my weaknesses but to acknowledge them, define them, and work with them. That's something many people struggle with, especially leaders. Many don't want to admit where they fall short. **But self-awareness is crucial.** The biggest challenge in managing people is getting them to recognize their blind spots. And when you make them aware and push them to acknowledge those gaps, that's when **real growth happens—through failure and vulnerability.**

In the journey of personal and professional growth, the acronym I have defined as **WAR—Weakness, Awareness, Recalibrate**—serves as a powerful framework for growth. Each component plays a vital role in transforming challenges into stepping stones for success. This chapter delves into the importance of understanding your weaknesses while simultaneously recognizing and leveraging your strengths.

Identifying weaknesses is often the most challenging part of self-awareness. Many shy away from this introspection, fearing the vulnerability of admitting flaws. Frankly, as human beings, we are all flawed, and the quicker we acknowledge those flaws, the quicker we can recalibrate to a more positive outlook. It's essential to remember that acknowledging weaknesses is not a sign of defeat; it's, in fact, the first step toward empowerment. It allows us to channel our efforts more effectively, transforming potential pitfalls into opportunities for growth.

Consider the wisdom in Will Smith's words: "You may be smarter than me, you may be better looking than me, but if you get on a treadmill next to me, you will get off before I do." This sentiment underscores a profound truth: perseverance is a strength that can overshadow many perceived advantages. Recognizing your weaknesses doesn't mean you're resigned to them; it means you can develop strategies to overcome them.

I often find it disheartening when I hear people talk about quitting. Quitting can seem like an easy way out, but it's frequently a symptom of deeper issues, like an inability to reflect on one's strengths and weaknesses. In today's world, where the allure of giving up is more prevalent than ever, it's essential to encourage a mindset of resilience. Those who take time to reflect can harness their strengths and use their weaknesses as catalysts for improvement, thereby overcoming barriers that might otherwise lead them to consider quitting.

Let me give you an example. Michael Jordan, renowned for his exceptional skills, competitive drive, and impact on the sport as a player and a cultural icon, was cut from his high school varsity basketball team as a sophomore. Jordan, who later became widely recognized as the greatest basketball player of all time, was told he wasn't good enough.

Instead of giving up, he put in the work day in, day out. He kept pushing, improving, and his junior year he made the varsity team. And look at what he became. What was his weakness back then? Simple—he hadn't developed his talents. But he didn't let that define him and certainly didn't quit. He turned his weakness into fuel, and the rest is history. Just imagine if Michael Jordan had decided to give up, my goodness.

Awareness is the bridge between recognizing weaknesses and harnessing strengths. It's about understanding who you are, both in terms of what you excel at and where you struggle. This duality is crucial. Many successful individuals don't ignore their weaknesses or allow them to hold them hostage. Instead, they recognize them clearly and use that knowledge to fuel their determination.

Through my experiences, I've learned that awareness fosters resilience. Being aware of my strengths has allowed me to refocus my energy when faced with setbacks. I often remind myself of my core abilities—my perseverance, tenacity, and refusal to quit. This self-awareness is an anchor amid chaos, reminding me that while I may stumble, I can rise again.

I have encountered many young adults who express feelings of inadequacy, often saying, "I don't have this" or "I don't have that." One case comes to mind: a young man who aspired to become a partner in his firm. Despite being younger and lacking the experience of his peers, he possessed a remarkable work ethic and energy that set him apart. In our discussions, we broke down his strengths and weaknesses, fostering a vulnerable space for growth. He realized that his unique qualities could overcome any perceived liabilities.

I remember that moment vividly; it made me smile. In his heart and mind, he knew what he had inside him to overcome challenges. He was the first to arrive at the office each morning and the last to leave at night. His unwavering work ethic allowed him to rise above his limitations. Later, he became a partner in the firm—an achievement that marked him as a trailblazer among his peers. Others would say, "If you want him, he will be there. He's a problem solver." His availability and dedication burned a lasting impression in their minds, proving that his **commitment was greater than any obstacle**.

Recalibration is where the magic happens. **It is what separates those who thrive from those who merely survive,** an individual bold enough to look themselves in the mirror, be aware of their weaknesses and recalibrate. Life is dynamic, and so are your challenges. Once you've identified your weaknesses and gained awareness of your strengths, the next step is to adapt and adjust your approach.

When you encounter adversity, ask yourself: How can this experience strengthen me? What can I learn from this setback? This mindset shift transforms obstacles into lessons, allowing you to recalibrate your path toward your goals. Remember, resilience is not just about bouncing back; it's about bouncing forward, using every setback as a springboard for future success.

Embracing the WAR framework can have a profound impact on your journey. By understanding your weaknesses, cultivating awareness, and recalibrating your strategies, you can enhance your resilience and perseverance, positioning yourself for long-term success. Never underestimate the power of getting back up after being knocked down. Your ability to adapt, learn, and grow will ultimately define your path to achievement. On the other hand, not being aware of your weaknesses means that you miss out on the opportunity to recalibrate, which can lead to misfires, distractions, and even derailments, ultimately preventing you from achieving your goals.

As we wrap up this chapter, I want to emphasize the importance of not quitting. As you define your utopia and chase your dreams, do so relentlessly and dream big. Embrace your strengths and be honest with yourself about your weaknesses. Use your strengths to overcome obstacles, because you were not put on this earth to be weak. Just as your body heals quickly from a cut, your mind and spirit can adapt and grow stronger.

Remember the quote I often share: "What lies ahead of you and what lies behind you pales in comparison to what lies within you." Your inner strength is a formidable force. Harness it, and let it guide you through every challenge you face.

Quotes:

"What lies ahead of you and what lies behind you pales in comparison to what lies within you."
~ Ralph Waldo Emerson

"I've failed over and over and over again in my life. And that is why I succeed." ~ Michael Jordan

"Success is not measured by what you accomplish, but by the opposition you have encountered, and the courage with which you have maintained the struggle against overwhelming odds."
~ Denzel Washington

"It is hard to beat the person who never gives up."
~ Babe Ruth

Premises:

- Growth occurs through failure and vulnerability.
- Let your commitment be greater than your obstacle.
- The ability to recalibrate your weaknesses separates those who thrive from those who merely survive.

Self-reflection questions:

- Can you boldly say what you are weak at?
- Are you willing to be vulnerable and open yourself up to the possibility of failure by facing your weaknesses?
- Are you prepared to work harder, consistently, and relentlessly than anyone else to transform your weaknesses into your biggest strengths?

Songs:

- "My Sacrifice" by Creed
- "Patience" by Guns N' Roses
- "Simple Man" by Lynryd Skynryd

CHAPTER 10

The End Game... ROAR

At the beginning of this book, I shared who it is for and what it aims to accomplish. I hope that you've taken away insights that make you a stronger, more capable person. Hopefully, you've found a few gems, "bits of honey," to help you grow and become more confident in yourself.

I've read many inspirational books, but too often, I've walked away without clear takeaways—no practical lessons to apply. That's why I end each chapter with premises, songs, and actionable items to ensure we are aligned and in sync in our journey. Let's do a quick recap before we move on to the **End Game...Roar**.

Chapter 1: Utopia as a Mindset

Is perfection attainable on Earth? Defining your Utopia and an unparalleled, tactical roadmap.

Chapter 2: SPEED, A path to holistic success

What is your tactical roadmap? How are you defining the areas where you will recreate a cadence to become a spiritual, physical, emotional economical and physical giant?

Chapter 3: Ordinary Becoming Extraordinary

Once you define Utopia as possible and create a tactical roadmap, how much commitment, energy, and endurance will you apply to that roadmap, to the credence? What are you prepared to do? No one can hold you back from achieving Utopia and becoming extraordinary but you.

Chapter 4: The Storm

Make no mistake, storms are coming. Are you equipped with your tactical roadmap? Do you have an established cadence? Are you going to let a storm define you, or are you going to be held back? Are you mentally prepared to understand the storm's severity, and is your foundation solid? When a storm hits, can you say one word—**Good**?

Chapter 5: Fear is a Liar

Fear, shame, and the past do funny things to people. Take risks, dream big, and have a strong nucleus to help you define and diffuse fear. Be bold, and mighty forces will come to your aid.

Chapter 6: Necessary Endings

A tough task mentally, but no doubt, pruning is absolutely needed. Pruning and managing relationships to ensure growth and the extraordinary is an absolute. You are the average of the five people you spend the most time with. Spend time with those who make a material impact on your goals. If you are the smartest, strongest person in the room, find a better room. To achieve utopia and become extraordinary, the people, the crowd, and the environment must have the same DNA. Don't get trapped in a cage and become the limp.

Chapter 7: Dream Big

Of course, everyone has their dreams. The dream may be simple, or as complex and challenging as flying to the moon. Dreaming big bleeds into defining your Utopia, creating your extraordinary. Most dreams fall short because of a lack of cadence, execution, and grit. You can't chase your dreams without a roadmap and the perseverance to see them through on the hardest of days.

Chapter 8: Don't Park Your Brain

Technology and AI are great tools for solving problems and creating efficiency, but they cannot replace our brain, cerebral horsepower, heart, soul, and thirst for human interaction and relationships. Technology is impacting our mental health and our relationships, and dumbing us down.

Chapter 9: WAR, Weakness, Awareness, Recalibration

Don't kid yourself. No human being is perfect and comes without weaknesses. Be strong enough, secure enough, and bold enough to identify and acknowledge your weaknesses. Be honest and vulnerable in reflection. Own your weaknesses as part of your DNA and view them not as obstacles, but as opportunities for growth.

Now that we have recapped, let's start the END GAME with another story.

I've mentioned my two cancer diagnoses. The first diagnosis was a trigger, a spark that helped me strengthen my mindset. The second diagnosis was February 13th, 2020, a month before the world stopped. I was in Fort Worth on an acquisition project when I started feeling severe back pain. My team urged me to go to the ER, but instead, I jumped in my truck and drove to Houston. Once there, I was told I had multiple tumors surrounding my kidneys and inferior vena cava.

Within days, I was at MD Anderson, one of the world's top cancer hospitals. The doctors told me the tumors were too close to the inferior vena cava for surgery to be an option. Instead, I would need high-dose chemotherapy.

Throughout this book, I've shared my journey of resilience—my pursuit of achieving my version of utopia. And now, 20 years and two months after my first diagnosis, I was facing cancer again. It would have been easy to fall into victimhood, to let this storm define me, but I refused. Three weeks later, COVID hit, and the entire healthcare system changed overnight. Hospitals became isolation zones. No visitors were allowed. Doctors and nurses walked around in full protective suits. I was alone, except for the poison being administered into my veins to kill the cancer.

During those months, I started organizing my thoughts for this book. I revisited the acronyms I had developed, trying to distill my journey into something clear and actionable for others to follow. I wanted to crystallize my experiences into a message that could strengthen those who read it.

For three months, I underwent chemotherapy. During that time, I kept asking myself: How will you let this storm impact you? That's when I developed the acronym ROAR, which I'll discuss shortly. I believe my second battle with cancer wasn't just another test—it was there to strengthen me even further, to sharpen my mind, to bring me closer to God, and to help me understand my ultimate purpose.

I've talked about being spiritually, physically, emotionally, economically, and developmentally fit—all of which contribute to achieving a life of meaning. This storm reinforced that vision for me. While I continue to focus on my career, physical strength, and economic well-being, I have realized that my spiritual impact on others has become the highest priority.

Today, I am cancer-free once again. The strange part? The tumors are still there. They couldn't be removed, but they've shrunk to just a centimeter and are now considered "benign" and not harmful. They are a constant reminder of the lessons I've memorialized in this book: Never let fear, adversity, or self-doubt take control of your soul. **Never feed the tumors.**

Another story that resulted in me recalibrating my SPEED and my utopia with more energy around the spiritual and developmental side was on an airplane.

I was on a flight, wearing a shirt for my nonprofit with the phrase "Always Changing Lives." A flight attendant noticed and asked about it. I explained our mission—how we raise money to help those battling cancer, veterans, and neighbors impacted by natural disasters. She shared that her mother was fighting cancer and struggling financially. I gave her access to our resources, and we discussed resilience, family, and finding strength in the face of adversity.

As the plane landed, I noticed the man sitting beside me—bigger than me, well over six feet, with thick arms and a long beard. As we stood to exit, he grabbed my arm firmly, looked me in the eye, and, with an Irish accent, said, "I heard what you said, mate. You're a flame—don't ever let it go out."

The flight attendant had tears in her eyes. That moment is burned into my memory. It reminded me why I do what I do.

Why I fight.

Why I share my story.

I believe wholeheartedly that we are all sons and daughters of a King—we must act like it! Live a life that reflects the character and values of a king, acting with grace, kindness, and authority as beneficiary of a royal lineage, not as a commoner; essentially, living with a sense of confidence, purpose, and love that comes from being part of a royal family. The only way to do that is to make every minute count—take advantage of every opportunity and view every challenge as a stepping stone toward reaching your utopia.

This phrase, "every minute counts," could not have been truer than during the COVID-19 pandemic, as we were all sequestered and secluded, watching as friends and family members became sick and sometimes passed away. Most of us had an eye-opening experience as loved ones were here one day and gone the next. While I was sitting at MD Anderson waiting to get chemo and had just been diagnosed with COVID, a fellow patient sitting next to me said, "Live it when you must live it." In other words, don't worry about it until you have to experience it. Of course, I encourage you to plan and be prepared, but unfortunately, there are some things you can never plan or prepare for. So, rather than worrying about them and the inevitability of the storms that will come, take advantage of every minute you are blessed to be walking on this earth and make every one of those minutes count.

As I sat there in isolation at MD Anderson, I developed the ROAR framework—a way to measure whether I was truly achieving my vision of success. The endgame is about assessing whether your puzzle pieces are coming together, so ROAR helps me evaluate my life appropriately.

R-Reflection: As you have read each chapter in this book, my hope, as mentioned in Chapter 9, is that you are engaging in solid reflection on how you become mentally and physically strong to achieve your utopia. Self-reflection is an exercise that should be done daily. As I sat at MD Anderson with cancer for the second time, I reflected on both positive and negative aspects in my life, challenges, wins, and obstacles I have overcome. Reflection is an integral part of growth and your pathway to Utopia.

O-Opportunity: What a powerful word. You, me, and all human beings have the same opportunity to achieve utopia and become extraordinary. It all depends on how we establish our credence, and cadence determines how successful we are with opportunities, to become wealthy, physically fit, a mental giant, and open a non-profit. Your life is full of opportunities. Again, as I sat at MD Anderson and reflected, I thanked God for the opportunities placed into my life and those to come.

A-Action and Accountability: Please, please, please be accountable to yourself. Hold your nucleus accountable and take action. Do not hesitate to establish a powerful credence to achieve Utopia. Again, as I reflected, I felt ashamed of letting minutes and seconds pass me by without taking action to enhance my opportunities. Create a tactical plan to take action; SPEED.

R-Radical: If you look up radical in the dictionary, **it's a change or action of the fundamental nature of something.** It is time for humans to look in the mirror and get radical about our utopia and cadence. I have been told a thousand times in my life that I am radical, radical in business, radical in fitness, radical in cadence, radical mentally. It's time for you to get radical around who and what you want to be.

As I rang the bell for my second cancer remission, I knew one thing for certain: This journey is not just about survival—it's about impact. When I reflect on my end game, one theme continues to emerge: leadership.

I've found myself stepping into leadership roles—personally, professionally, and spiritually—without even realizing it. This has happened organically as a result of striving for excellence, and being radical. When you push yourself to achieve the extraordinary and carry the DNA of resilience and determination, leadership is inevitable.

Although you may wake up to realize that you have allowed life to carry you this way or that, if you are still breathing, it is not too late to heed the warning. My mother, for example, is a working mom for thirty years who decided to make the most of her time now that she had raised her children.

After retiring, she began visiting this nail salon, where she befriended the owner, Tony. She and Tony started to hang out, having lunch, and going on different adventures. Suddenly, to everyone's surprise, she started getting tattoos. When we questioned her about her decisions during what we called "later in life," she replied, "Every minute counts, so now I'm taking advantage of my life." And why not?

In ancient Greece, they didn't list a person's accomplishments upon their passing. Obituaries weren't about achievements—they were about the fire within.

Did they truly live?

Were they passionate?

That was the real measure of a life well-lived. What does a well-lived life look like to you, and what are you doing to ensure it comes to fruition?

I will step off my pedestal and leave you to ponder after this last analogy—**The Chinese Bamboo Story**.

Feeling defeated by life, a frustrated man exiled himself in the woods, where he met a hermit. Desperate, he asked, "Give me one good reason not to quit."

The hermit pointed to two plants: a fern and a bamboo. "I nurtured both. The fern quickly grew, but the bamboo took years to show any sign of life. Yet, after four years of hidden growth, it shot up a hundred feet in just six months."

"Did the bamboo lie dormant?" asked the hermit. The man realized that while he struggled, he also built a strong foundation for his future. Inspired, he returned to pursue his dreams with renewed persistence.

The Chinese bamboo tree is a powerful metaphor for personal growth and success, illustrating that while progress may seem slow and invisible, persistence will lead to significant breakthroughs. The bamboo narrative proves it's never too late, it sits underground for 3 years before it explodes 80 feet. A strong cadence and foundation will require discipline before significant fruit is produced. Many people seek quick fixes and shortcuts for success, but such solutions are often unsustainable and temporary. Remembering the lessons from the bamboo tree can motivate us during frustrating times, reminding us that real growth takes time and dedication. **Don't be one of the many; be one of the few who sacrifice and achieve their dreams. The ripest peach is at the top of the tree**.

Quotes:

"What lies ahead of you and what lies behind you pales in comparison to what lies within you."
~ Ralph Waldo Emerson

"If not now, when?" ~ Hillel the Elder

"There is no try, do or do not." ~ Yoda

"Gather ye rosebuds while ye may." ~ Robert Herrick

Premises:

- Have enough courage to look yourself in the mirror.
- Ensure a strong and solid foundation so the opportunity is not missed.
- Go on a radical reckoning!
- Don't give up. The bamboo cultivates unnoticed for 3 years without any sign of life before dramatic growth.

Self-reflection questions:

- Are you looking at yourself in the mirror?
- If not now, when?
- How loud will your ROAR be?
- Do you have a cadence to follow, and are you persistent with your activity?

Songs:

- "Son of a Sinner" by Jelly Roll
- "Schism" by Tool
- "If today was your last day" by Nickelback
- "I Hope This Gets to You" by The Daylights
- "Beautiful Things" by Benson Boone
- "We Will Rock You" by Queen

Thank you and Acknowledgments

Thank you for taking the time to read this book. If you've made it this far, I believe I can now greet you as a friend. The stories within these pages are deeply rooted in my family and friends— my nucleus—without whom I would not be who I am today or have achieved the success I enjoy. My father, mother, brothers, children, and a handful of close friends have been instrumental in shaping my journey. While I throw a few jabs and humorous anecdotes, please know that these loved ones have played a vital role in my growth and accomplishments. Their unwavering support, laughter, and lessons have made this story possible, and I am forever grateful for their presence in my life.